Stress to Joy

Your Toolkit to Restore Peace of Mind in Minutes

Gary,
May the light inside you shine on people around you.
Rozina

Dr. Rozina Lakhani   11/26/19

Bridge
Books

Stress to Joy: Your Toolkit to Restore Peace of Mind in Minutes.

978-0-9984007-0-9
Published by Bridge Books.

Cover design by Awais Shahzad

Published by Bridge Books
Printed in the United States of America

Dedication

Dedicated to His Highness Shah Karim
Alhussaini Aga Khan, Imam (spiritual leader)
of the Ismaili Muslims, whose 60 years of
leadership in the fields of development
including global health, education,
microfinance, built environment, and
pluralism has made a difference in the lives of
millions of people worldwide.

He is a beacon of light and a source of
inspiration for me.

Claim your support material

http://stresstojoy.com/resources

Stress to Joy is not just a book. It is a toolkit to aid you on your transformational journey from stress to joy.

To help you do the exercises in this book, I have created a number of supporting resources that accompany the processes you'll experience in this book, including downloadable worksheets and audio exercises.

These are included free as my gift to help you create the happiness you desire and deserve.

Praise for Stress to Joy

*"Stress to Joy is a fantastic book!
The concept of 'advanced gratitude' and the
action plan for implementing this practice in
daily life really resonated with me. It is a very
simple, but powerful technique. I also love the
analogy of stress as traffic lights. This offers a
very useful visual. I LOVE the CPR acronym!*

*This book truly inspired me to take a look at my
own stress and to re-evaluate my routines. This
manuscript presents a good mix of novel content
and a fresh view and interpretation of time-tested
stress reduction approaches.*

*Thank you for this beautiful gift of information
and skill building practices!"*
Tatiana Sadak Ph.D. PMHNP. ARNP

*"This is not just an impressive book, it is a
spectacular one ... It can only be described as a
carefully crafted, step by step guide, with
everyday examples, to help the reader relate and
apply simple techniques to cross the bridge from
stress to joy.*

*A simple recipe to transform (stressful) life by
inculcating small shifts in perspective that bring*

huge rewards! I recommend this book to anyone who has room for joy in their life." **Nadia Huda.**

"Awesome! It is very relatable and does make me step back and think." **Shyna Dhanani.**

"I like how familiar and caring Dr. Rozina is with her readers. It feels like she is talking to the reader. Not only does she share anecdotes about herself but also why she had a difficult time doing an exercise and what she did to make it better. Very helpful!" **Jean Tracy, MSS**

"This book is amazing, all the stories, and examples are great. Especially the comparison between milk and water made me cry. I feel that you wrote this book for me. All the examples and techniques seem simple to follow." **Shirin Halani.**

"I thought this book really addressed the issues that working women face on a daily basis. The information in your book will help many professionals understand the importance of self-care to be resilient and joyful." **Jane Small ARNP**

"You have made your message fun. Your writing is light, sometimes humorous, and very real. It was an easy read, which is what many readers are looking for these days." **Gloria Harrison Psy. D**

"Stress to Joy is a practical book. It gave me helpful tips to help me when I feel overwhelmed with life responsibilities. I use the 'Brain Dump Bubble' or the '5 Ds for Prioritizing' to clear the clutter in my mind.

I also felt empowered by using tools like the 'Self-Dialogue Journal' to clear my thoughts, the 'Gratitude Journal', which helps me to focus on the positives in my life, and the 'Emotional Coping Account' to help me stay balanced." **Lydia Hathaway.**

About the Author

Dr. Rozina Lakhani's mission is to promote health and happiness. She works as a psychiatrist at Shifa Health, a clinical professor at the University of Washington and Medical Director at Residence XII Women Drug Treatment Program.

She is also a member of the American Stress Institute and offers talks and trainings to various groups.

Dr. Rozina received her medical degree from the Aga Khan University in Pakistan and completed her Master of Public Health degree and her residency in Psychiatry from the University of Illinois in Chicago. She is a diplomate of American Board of Psychiatry and Neurology.

Today, Dr. Rozina lives with her husband and 2 children in the Pacific Northwest.

She is passionate about helping people reduce stress and dreams of a world where people pursue a happy life with love and purpose.

Gratitude - Dr. Rozina Says:

I am happy and grateful for all the people who have influenced my life. Many of you have told your stories, revealed your wisdom and given me support. Thank you for helping me share these simple, practical and powerful tools.

I would especially like to thank: my family, who supported and encouraged me, (my parents, Ramzan Ali and Sherbanoo, my husband, Jalal, and my children, Rumi and Ruhi) and my friends and colleagues who shared their wisdom, inspiration and insightful feedback (with special mention of Jean Tracy, Nadia Huda, Gloria Harrison, Linda Petit, Khadeeja Jan Mohammad, and Shams Juma).

Thank you to my coaches Derek Doepker, Ben & Suzanne Patwa, Christine Closer and the many teachers throughout my life, and my patients who gracefully allowed me to be part of their life journey and who continue to inspire me.

To all of you who have crossed my path, thank you!

Table of Contents

Introduction :

Why Choose Stress to Joy

Stress to Joy

Hello. How are you?

Did you answer, "I am fine" and mean it, or did your mind say, "You have no idea how stressed I feel?"

Of course, I cannot feel the stress that you feel because your feelings are unique to you. But I can still share what I have learned from my life and the lives of the people I've had the privilege of helping, in my psychiatry practice, my seminars, or within my community.

I have seen that everyone faces stressful life situations. Some can cope very well and turn that stress into an opportunity. They feel joy, peace, and happiness. But many are unable to do so. They suffer from stress, and it morphs into various types of illnesses. For almost two decades in my psychiatry practice, I have observed lives being damaged by stress.

In this book, I can share what I have seen in my work to try to help you minimize the stress and maximize the joy in your life.

Since I specialize in the treatment of severe depression, many people come to me after suffering for a long time and trying numerous treatments. My heart aches when I see a patient like Marla.

Marla is a tall and healthy-looking woman in her 40s. A few years before she came to see me, she had a happy but very busy and stressful life with her job, kids, family, and social commitments.

She was too busy to attend to herself, and the stress started manifesting in the form of headaches, insomnia, and irritability. She did not even realize that her stress had progressed into clinical depression.

She started getting so emotional and irritable that her marriage was on the verge of collapse, and she almost lost her job.

She finally realized it when she started having suicidal thoughts. She loved her family and did not want to die. She felt scared and finally came for treatment. Because her symptoms were already severe, we had to use advanced treatment methods.

It's impossible to simply eliminate stress. It is best to teach people how to harness their stress to positive ends. For this reason, we had to also work on Marla's mental training.

This training helped her change the way she faced the stressful situations in her life so she could prevent getting sick again and fully enjoy her life.

She understood that some causes of ill health are not in her control (e.g., genetics and environment), but some are (e.g., how she responds to various challenges/stressors in her life).

She learned that the ways she coped with stress made a huge difference in both causing the illness and healing from it. Do you think Marla would have suffered less if she had an opportunity to get this training before her stress got out of control?

I see patients like Marla day in and day out. I see the havoc caused by uncontrolled stress: broken marriages, suffering kids, depression, anxiety, alcohol and drug addiction, heart attacks, strokes, and more.

Therefore, I feel a responsibility to save people from reaching those severe stages as much as possible. My hope is that everyone can be the very best versions of themselves.

It would not only help them suffer less and enjoy more, but it would also impact the people around them, and that ripple effect can spread peace and happiness.

When I realize how simple practices, techniques, and shifts in mindsets can make a huge difference in someone's ability to overcome illness and be healthy and happy, I feel the calling to bring this training to people before they get sick and suffer.

When I work with organizations that are concerned about the increasing rates of suicide, I try to convince them that they can make a bigger impact if they focus on the mental training necessary to healthily handle stress. By the time a person develops severe depression or suicidal thoughts, the clock is ticking.

Although it is never too late, the training is much easier and faster to learn and implement before someone develops complications from stress.

I often joke in my seminars, "I am teaching you these techniques so you don't have to become my patient." However, there's nothing wrong with seeking psychiatric help. If you can learn to train your mind earlier, you can save yourself from a lot of unnecessary suffering.

I want to help you train your mind so you can manage stressful situations, reshape challenges into opportunities for growth, enjoy each day of your life, laugh with family, feel productive, and be the best you can be.

I believe that life is a beautiful journey with many winding roads, changing scenarios, and traffic lights. These are all going to be there, whether you enjoy them or get stressed by them.

Have you noticed the difference? When you are in a vacation mindset, you enjoy the changing scenarios with excitement, observe the world with curiosity, and don't get bothered by the traffic lights. But when you are rushing to your next appointment, the same roads, environment, and traffic lights become stressful. Why? It's all because of a different mindset. The way you approach and adjust to changing circumstances make a huge difference.

Is it possible to change your mindset?

The answer becomes clear when you consider a computer analogy. Your computer has two components. One is the physical machine—the hardware that you can see. The second is the programming—the software that you can't see.

This invisible software makes the computer perform in a certain manner. What do you do when your computer is not working at its best?

When my computer starts working slowly or giving me trouble, my tech support has taught me to clear the cache and update my applications.

Even when it is running well, I need to run maintenance from time to time to clean, update, and reprogram it to get the best possible performance.

In this analogy, the brain is the physical hardware, while the mind is the invisible software that runs the hardware of brain and body. You need to clear, update, and reprogram it from time to time to keep it performing at its best. This book is going to help you do that.

This is not just any book. It is the result of many years of experience, inspiration, and application.

Although I've had many years of education and learning from my patients, these tools have taken on a very personal meaning since I try many of these techniques myself.

I experience stress, firsthand.

Being a mother, a professional businesswoman, and an active volunteer in my community, my life has so many demands that the word "busy" doesn't begin to describe it.

When people ask me if my life is busy, I answer, "My life is very colorful; there is never a dull moment." These colors keep life interesting, but sometimes they become too much. I refer to them as traffic lights on the road of life.

Sometimes the lights are green, and life is flowing smoothly.

Sometimes they are yellow, and I have to slow down or put pressure on the brakes to get through the crossroads.

Sometimes they are red, and I have to stop.

Sometimes they are malfunctioning and cause a traffic jam. It takes longer, and I need additional help from someone to direct the traffic. But no matter how bad or how long, the traffic starts flowing again.

Like everyone, I have to go through many of these lights/stressful periods in my life too.

The longest and most significant one came when I broke my right hand in a car accident. If you've ever experienced loss of function, especially in your dominant hand, you may be able to relate to how stressful it is when you can't perform basic activities in life like zipping your pants, opening food jars, or taking care of yourself and your family.

Although that was the most difficult time of my life, I can say that it was also a huge opportunity for personal growth. I had to train my mind and practice the techniques I teach to get through that challenging time.

When I started getting better, I wanted to share these techniques with everyone. I started jotting down "aha moments", techniques, and perspectives I found that worked. I made a special folder on my laptop for these insights, and they became the basis for the program and this book, "Stress to Joy."

I have seen how these simple techniques have helped my patients, my friends, and me. Now I am very happy and grateful to share them with you.

Why read this book when there are so many others?

There is no deficit of information out there. In fact, there is too much conflicting information with countless gaps. It is stressful even trying to figure out how to manage stress. Therefore, I wrote this book.

Just as a bridge connects, fills the gaps, and provides a path from one place to another, in this book I have attempted to combine the ideas from different approaches, fill the gaps between *what* and *how,* and help you move from a state of stressful-ness to a state of joyful-ness—simply stress to joy.

Many books focus on a single aspect of managing stress. When you focus on only one characteristic, many times the benefits don't sustain. I believe that unless you train your mind to stop generating stress, it keeps producing more.

In this book, I am going to help you train your brain from several angles so you can respond to your circumstances in a way that produces less stress and more joy.

Although one system can't take care of everything, this training can address many major issues specifically due to your unhealthy reaction to stress. Your perspective will change your stressors from sources of illness to opportunities for growth.

This program will take you one step further than just managing stress. When you only focus on getting rid of stress, your focus remains on pain. You don't feel "really good," you just feel "less bad." Therefore, don't stop at reducing stress only but continue to develop happiness habits.

The way you handle life's challenges affects your level of joy, and your level of joy affects how you handle stress. They are two sides of the coin, and your inner joy can cut down the negative effect of stress, which is beautifully depicted on the book's cover.

As you read through this book, you may feel that you know some of these techniques but not others. Use this book as a reminder to practice. Sometimes one technique may work, and another time, you may need a different one.

A single tool cannot fix every problem, and you need different tools at different times. Consider this book as your mental skills "toolkit."

You can pick a specific tool for the different situations as they arise.

An important point to remember here is that even the best toolkit may not have the tools necessary for all situations, so you may need to find extra tools as needed.

Similarly, although this book has tools that may fill your basic toolkit—which you can use in 50-75% of situations—sometimes additional treatment will be necessary.

Therefore, I urge you to seek further professional guidance, when needed, even while you are working on helping yourself with these tools.

Do you know how many people think about doing something to improve their lives but don't take any steps? You took your first step on this journey from stress to joy by picking up this book.

Therefore, I commend you for investing your time and energy in your health and happiness. I feel grateful to you for letting me be your guide and companion on this transformational journey.

If you follow through and apply even some of the techniques suggested here, I think you will be able to minimize your stress and maximize your joy.

But if you don't monitor and improve your mindset as needed, the stressors may creep back up and result in a loss of joy and increased suffering.

So, let's start your journey. In the following chapters, you will learn the tools to help you on this path in a systematic manner through the examples of three of my good friends.

Although I have changed their names and details for privacy and ease of learning, these are real-life experiences.

I specifically chose the stories of my friends who are not suffering from any mental illness to emphasize the point that anyone can use these techniques.

They will help you learn a stress-to-joy system to transform any stress from a source of suffering to an opportunity for growth. You deserve to feel the joy and peace in life.

Ready? Lets's begin with the first step; Acknowledge.

Chapter 1
Acknowledge:

How to figure out where you are so you can get where you want to go.

Do you find that theoretical concepts make more sense when you see how someone is able to apply them in her real life? Let me introduce you to my friends. Sam, Rene, and Natasha share how they were able to apply these tools on their journeys from stress to joy. The steps will be evident within the acronym **ACR**. What is **A**? It's the first step.

Sam

Sam is a single woman in her thirties. She works as a director of finance for a midsize company. She acknowledged one day, when we met at a community gathering, that she was feeling stressed and overwhelmed due to her extra-long commute. She was spending 90 minutes each way, 5 days a week, in addition to more than 10 hours a day at work (a total of more than 65 hours a week).

She didn't have time for exercise or art, which were her usual outlets, and the stress was making her skin condition worse.

She wanted to feel happy and stress-free so she could enjoy time with her family.

Rene

Rene is a married woman in her fifties. She works as a mortgage broker. She acknowledged one day on the phone that she was feeling stressed and overwhelmed due to the demands of her many clients.

She was meticulous about completing all the paperwork needed to close the mortgages on time. Feeling overwhelmed was affecting her productivity and her frustration tolerance. She was getting irritated with her family.

She was stuck in a cycle of emotional eating. When I asked her what she would be doing differently if she was less stressed, she said that she would feel relaxed, work with focus, eat healthily, and enjoy her loved ones. She wanted to change because she valued her work and her family.

Natasha
Natasha is another very good friend of mine. She is a married woman in her forties with three kids, a husband, a highly demanding job in the IT industry, and a very involved community life.

On top of those, she is a perfectionist.

She acknowledged one day that the stress was causing her back pain and sleep difficulties as her mind kept spinning with issues that worried or angered her. She noticed that she was getting easily irritated with her family and coworkers. She wanted to feel calm again and improve her relationships. She valued her health and her family's happiness.

These three women were able to start their journeys from stress to joy once they acknowledged where they were, where they wanted to be, and why.

Therefore, the journey of transformation from stress to joy starts with **acknowledgment**.

It seems obvious that you'd need to acknowledge the issue before you can solve it? But you would be surprised how many people go through life without acknowledging their body's signals. Somehow, we get trained to behave like machines while competing in this meritocratic society. We learn to suppress our feelings.

Many people think that acknowledging the fact that they are feeling overwhelmed or worried is acknowledging that they are weak and cannot handle the pressure. Really? Is it weaker to acknowledge your feelings so you can take steps to improve, or to suppress the feelings until you break down?

Notice, observe, and become aware, so you can acknowledge how you feel. Name your feeling, as these feelings are an indicator of the balance in your **Emotional Coping Account.**

What is an Emotional Coping Account (ECA)? It is an internal, emotional account that we all have. Your feelings are the alert system for this account. You get alerts from your bank when your bank balance goes below a certain amount.

Similarly, when the balance in your ECA drops, you get stress signals in the form of negative feelings. If you don't attend to it, it starts manifesting in the form of body symptoms.

The higher the balance in ECA, the better you feel—the lower the balance, the worse you feel.

You need to respond by taking action. If you are feeling stress and overwhelmed, they are your signals that you may have a low balance in your Emotional Coping Account. Acknowledge them. Tell yourself that it is okay to feel the feelings. You just need to take some steps to bring the balance back to positive.

Question 1: What are *your* feelings now? Are they indicating a positive or negative balance in your emotional coping account?

_____

_____

_____

Like any bank account, the balance in this Emotional Coping Account is affected by the amounts of withdrawals and deposits.

Everything that makes you feel bad is a withdrawal from this account.

This includes all of the outside stressful situations and your reactions that drain you and make you feel stressed.

Everything that makes you feel good is your deposit.

That includes good things that may happen to you or your internal response in the form of what you feel, say, and do that energize you and make you feel joy.

Withdrawals
Sam's withdrawals (stressors) were her commuting hours, not eating/drinking/sleeping at the right time, and how she was reacting to her work demands. Rene's withdrawals were her need to meet the timelines for multiple clients and how she was prioritizing or not prioritizing her time.

Natasha's withdrawals were her multiple demands and her need for perfection leading to a difficult relationship with coworkers and family. These are some of the common stressors most people face.

In research done by the American Psychological Association, American Institute of Stress, NY, published July 8, 2014; people identified the following seven most common stressors:

1. **Job Pressures** (tension with coworkers, bosses, and work overload)

2. **Money** (loss of job, reduced retirement, medical expenses)

3. **Health** (health crisis, terminal or chronic illness)

4.   **Relationships** (divorce, death of spouse, arguments with friends, loneliness)

5.   **Poor Nutrition** (inadequate nutrition, caffeine, processed foods, refined sugars)

6.   **Media Overload** (television, radio, the Internet, email, social networking)

7.   **Sleep Deprivation** (inability to release adrenaline and other stress hormones)

Question 2: What are *your* withdrawals?

_____

_____

_____

Deposits

For your bank account balance to stay positive, your deposits have to be higher than your withdrawals.

You know what happens if your withdrawals increase more than your balance and your deposits don't grow to match.
Your account becomes negative, right? Your checks bounce and you have to pay the penalty.
So, what do prudent people do?
They make regular deposits and keep a reserve as an emergency fund. For situations when there are unexpected withdrawals, the reserve can save them from going into the negative.

When there is so much happening to us from the outside that's not in our control, sometimes we forget what is still *in* our control.

Although some of the withdrawals may not be in our control, many deposits are.

Sam identified that art and exercise were her deposits. Rene identified listening to music, writing in her journal, and taking a tub bath as her deposits. Natasha identified that taking some quiet time sitting by her window, meditation, and socializing with her friends were her deposits. She had to be selective about how she socialized since some of her friends consider alcohol as one of their deposits. She knows that although alcohol may temporarily numb her feelings, it also blurs her thinking, causes disinhibition and makes people do things that they regret. Therefore, alcohol is a withdrawal, and not a deposit, in the long run.

Question 3: What are *your* deposits?

_____

_____

_____

It is such an important question but most people keep living their lives without knowing what their deposits are.

Make a list and keep it in an accessible place, because when you are feeling down it can be hard to remember.

You can download an example of an emotional coping account balance sheet and deposit list as well as blank worksheets at http://stresstojoy.com/resources

Setting the GPS Destination
Answering the previous three questions will allow you to acknowledge where you are (your starting point).

To get anywhere, you'll also need to decide where you want to go. The clearer the destination, the higher the chances that you will make it.

Sam wanted to decrease her skin inflammation, feel stress-free, and enjoy her work and personal life. Rene wanted to stop emotional eating, control her irritability, and enjoy her work and family. Natasha wanted to decrease her back pain, sleep well, and enjoy her relationships.

She wanted to look forward to things with a smile on her face.

Question 4: What does *your* destination look like? What would you like to be feeling, thinking, saying, or doing by taking this journey from stress to joy?

_____

_____

As you are identifying your destination goal, let me share a technique that I stumbled upon which can increase your chances of achieving any goal in life.

You may have heard about affirmations and visualization as powerful techniques. What are they?

When you say a positive, short statement in the present tense, your intentions—as if you have already achieved them—are called affirmations.

Visualization is simply seeing those things in your mind's eye as vividly as if they already happened.

Because your brain can be prepared for achieving goals, these affirmations and visualizations are like seeds that you sow in your mind's field.

They provide a trailer to the mind for what you want so it can move toward your desires.

Have you ever felt a little flustered when you turn on the TV and a movie is playing, but you have no idea what it's about?

Sometimes it is okay, but most of the time your brain takes a few moments to make sense of what is going on in the story.

Your brain likes it better when it has some idea.

When you check out the name, description, or trailer, your brain gets ready, knows what is coming, and can more thoroughly enjoy the movie.

Similarly, before doing anything, if you set an intention and visualize the destination, it gives your brain a framework, a blueprint, and a file folder in which to put the information.

When the documentary *The Secret* by Rhonda Byrne came out in 2006, I did not question the "power of attraction" because I knew the power of affirmations and visualization.

I liked Bob Proctor's suggestion in that documentary when he suggested writing affirmations with the prompt, "I am so happy and grateful that I have... [whatever you want, but don't yet have]."

I tried his suggestion, but I had one little problem. My logical mind could not accept the notion of: "Just believe it, even if your mind questions it," as one of the speakers suggested in that documentary.

It felt like a lie, and if your mind doesn't accept what you say, then those words hold no power for you.

How can I just believe that I have enough money in my bank account when my bank statement shows otherwise? How can I think that I can pay the bills when I'm getting collection calls?

Just imagine what would happen if you assumed that you had enough money, and you wrote a check despite your bank account not having sufficient funds to cover it. Of course, the check would bounce, and you would have to pay the bank fees.

As I was contemplating the issue, I came across the phrase "Advanced Gratitude" written somewhere, and I had an "aha moment."

I thought about the fact that I pay rent to live in an apartment, pay for the groceries before taking them home, and write "thanking you in advance" when asking someone for a favor in a letter.
What if I give thanks for things I want before getting them? My mind accepted that.

So, I started writing in my journal, "I offer advanced gratitude that *I am* or *I have*..." or whatever I wanted.

That was my affirmation. I started to see it in my mind's eye as if it had happened, and it became a powerful tool for me.

Sometimes those things came true for me within days, and sometimes they came true after years, and some have still not come true. Either they are not right for me or the right time has not come.

Either way, my writing keeps reminding me of my intention and motivates me to keep taking action toward my desired goals, increasing the chances of achieving those objectives.

For example, "I offer advanced gratitude that I am happy; I have a healthy, energetic, and functional body; I can keep balance in my life; I am making a difference in millions of lives with my writing."

Just adding the phrase "I offer advanced gratitude" before Bob Proctor's suggested prompt allowed me to connect my logical mind with the power of focusing on the things I wanted.

Since then, I have been using this prompt as a part of my daily journal, and I reap the benefits of affirmations and visualizations without my mind questioning it.

I invite you to journal your desired destination on this journey with the prompt:

"I offer advanced gratitude for __W i s d o m__

_____."

Finding the Purpose/Motivator
Many times, people say they want to change, but they don't.

Why?

Either they are not ready or are not truly convinced that they need to. They don't have a clear motivation. Sam's skin condition was her big motivator.

Rene's increasing weight was convincing her that she needed to change. Natasha's back pain was motivating her.

You don't have to wait for a big signal from your body to motivate you. You can choose to avoid possible suffering and manage your stress before it manages you.

According to one of the estimates, stress contributes to 70-90% of health care visits.

These are not only mental conditions like depression and anxiety, but many physical conditions like heartburn, migraine, high blood pressure, irritable bowel, and even heart attacks and strokes are related to stress.

In fact, it's hard to think of any disease in which stress does not play an aggravating role.

In addition to health, stress also takes a toll on our energy, productivity, brilliance, and creativity.

According to The American Institute of Stress, "Stress is considered America's #1 problem, and in 2003, stress was estimated to cost US businesses $300,000,000,000/year! Every year the impact is increasing exponentially.

Question 5: What is *your* motivation? Why do you want to invest your time and thought into transforming your stress and building your happiness?

To be wise is the Energy Transforming factor

By answering these five questions, you have taken your first step on the journey from a state of stress to a state of joy. Before you proceed, let me answer some questions that may be surfacing in your mind—like **how stress can cause so many problems,** especially conditions like heart attacks, high blood pressure, pain, or skin conditions.

Your body is intrinsically set to face stressors and challenges for its safety and proper functioning. For example, when you are driving and you see someone crossing the road, your body is programmed to react.

Your eyes see, your brain sends signals to your muscles to contract, and your foot pushes the brake pedal. You avoid an accident.

Your body took action to protect you. You may continue to feel your heart beating, shallow respirations, or tense muscles for a few minutes, but your body comes back to normal.

This normal state of the body is called homeostasis in medical terms—a return to balance.

Let me share, in more scientific detail, how the brain processes the aforementioned situation.

The three main parts of the brain involved in this process are your Cortex (the CEO or "control center" of the brain), Limbic System— the amygdala and the hippocampus— (the emotional center of the brain), and Reticular Activating System or RAS (the filter of the brain).

In the example, when you saw the pedestrian step onto the street, the nerve cells in your eyes picked up the signal and sent it to the cortex.

On the way, that signal was modified. The emotional center attached the fear associated with similar situations from past learnings.

The filter system cut out the unnecessary detail of all the other events happening around you and brought attention to the most important event—the pedestrian stepping onto the street.

Your cortex analyzed the signal as a danger (stress) and came into action. Your cortex ordered your leg muscles to contract and push the brakes. It also ordered the adrenal glands to produce more cortisol, which increased your heart rate and pushed more blood to the muscles of your feet so they could contract.

In essence, your brain perceived, your body followed, and you prevented an accident.

Once you resolve the issue, the cortex orders the body to calm down, your heart rate slowly returns to normal, your blood pressure reduces, your body and mind get back to normal, and you move on.

Similarly, whenever your brain deems a signal as a danger, the amygdala, as part of your emotional system, acts as an alarm and leads to the fight-flight-freeze response. When there is an external challenge, this alarm gets triggered.

It is for your protection (like preventing an accident). Once the danger passes, the body and mind are supposed to calm down and reset the stress alarm.

However, when any mechanical system is excessively used, it malfunctions. Similarly, with excess use and poor maintenance, your amygdala can also malfunction.

When it is activated too frequently and doesn't get enough time to cool down, it starts giving signals even when there is no danger.

Just imagine how annoying it would be if an alarm system kept going on all the time or at the wrong times.

In addition to being annoying, there are also physiologic effects from these frequent stress signals.

When the stress signals are continuous or frequent, the cortisol level in the body doesn't get the chance to return to normal.

The initial cortisol increase is meant to increase the pressure in blood vessels so more blood can go to your leg muscles and you can respond to the stress—like the need to prevent the accident. But when the cortisol level stays high for a long time, so does your blood pressure, and you develop high blood pressure.
When your muscles stay contracted for too long, they start hurting. You feel the tension and develop chronic pain.

When the blood supply to the brain is affected, it results in headaches, and in severe cases, may result in a stroke.

Furthermore, as the blood gets directed to your muscles, the supply to your gut goes down. When the blood doesn't go to your gut for some time, you start having diarrhea or constipation.

You may develop irritable bowel syndrome. Cortisol also increases the acid production in your stomach, which results in heartburn. You may develop acidity or ulcers. When the blood supply to the skin decreases, it may cause skin problems.

If the blood vessels going to your heart are squeezed, you can have a heart attack.

A simple protective mechanism can transform into a stress-induced illness.

Not only can stress reaction produce illness, but it also leads to further stress. This starts a vicious cycle. For example, you may have the stress of bills that are larger than your paycheck. You may start worrying about it so much that you are not able to sleep.

This lack of sleep may lead to tiredness and an inability to function at your best, compromising your job, affecting your income, and causing additional stress.

Or you become more irritable, you scream at your loved ones, and that causes relationship stress. You get stuck in an ongoing cycle of stress.

Stress——>Reaction——>Stress

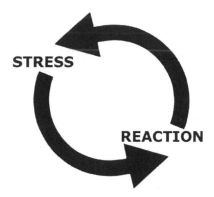

A continuous stress cycle, when not broken from time to time, can lead to depression or anxiety, especially if there are other risk factors present.

Sometimes people ask, "If stress is so prevalent and it can have such devastating effects, why do some people become stronger when faced with a similar stressor?"

Well, it depends on both the amount of stress and the person's capacity to respond. Just as a stretchy rubber band regains its form due to its elasticity, your mind can recover from a stress attack due to its resilience.

"Resilience" is that flexibility, elasticity, and immunity that helps you bounce back after a stressor strikes, stopping it from overwhelming you. You can increase your resilience with mental training.

Resilience can give you freedom from stress. Freedom doesn't mean a total absence of stress. Although, when you are tired of the stress, it is natural to wish for it all to disappear.

But that is not practical. Freedom from stress doesn't mean that there are no stressors; it means that despite the stressors, you don't experience **feeling stressed**.

You are not the prisoner of stress. Stress no longer burdens you. You are not fighting it, but dancing with it. You can happily coexist with all the stressors. You are managing your stress before it manages you.

You are transforming it into an opportunity for growth.

How can stress be an opportunity? You *need* some stress to propel you in the right direction.

You may have noticed that without any stress you lose some of your motivation. But with the right amount of pressure, you are more likely to get the work done.

That ideal intensity of challenges is necessary for your growth. For example, when you exercise with the right amount of weights, you can build your muscles.

On the other hand, you can injure the same muscles if you try to lift weights that are more than your muscles can handle. You can build your muscle capacity by training.

The weight you use to train is a stress on your muscle but becomes an opportunity to grow stronger.

Sometimes you try a technique a few times and say, "This doesn't work." Do you attempt a physical exercise a few times and say, "This doesn't work" when you don't see immediate results?

No, you try to find a good trainer who can take you through the steps and introduce suitable tools at appropriate stages to increase your muscle capacity for greater challenges without injury.

Similarly, with the right tools and gradual guidance, you can train your mind and build your emotional resilience.

If the demands and pressures come faster than your capacity at a particular time, you will experience stress-related conditions. You can't control what stressful life situations arise, but you can gradually increase your resilience and capacity to handle whatever comes at you.

You can't change something that you don't notice, so the first step on this training journey is to acknowledge. You took that step by answering the questions in this chapter. If you haven't written down your answers, go ahead and do that now.

You can also download this questionnaire at http://stresstojoy.com/resources.

If you acknowledge how you are feeling, you will have the power to decide if you want to change or not. If you don't acknowledge, you may continue to suffer, stuck in a stress cycle.

Now that you have taken the first step, are you ready to take the next step to break your stress cycle? If you have acknowledged your starting balance in your emotional coping account (starting point), how you want to feel (destination), and why (motivation), then you are ready for the next step, **C** in the acronym **ACR**, which will be described in the next chapter.

Chapter 2

Calm:

*How to relax your mind
when there is so much going on.*

Is your mind still pretty worked up and your body still reacting? You have taken the first step towards acknowledging your stress, but now you need to calm down. Without a calm mind, you can't think properly.

Without a calm body, you can't function properly. What can you do? Let's see what our friends did next to cope with their stress.

Sam
Since Sam took her new job as a controller, her level of responsibility and her commute had both increased. She no longer had time for exercise or art, which were two activities that used to help her de-stress.

She could change her job, but that was a long-term solution, which takes time. Until she could find an alternative to create a better work-life balance, she needed something to immediately implement within her busy schedule.

Her commute kept her on the road for almost three hours per day. She asked, "What can I do? There isn't much I can accomplish while driving. I can't walk around or do any artistic activity.

There are not even scenic views to enjoy on the expressway!"

I asked her if she practices mindfulness while driving. She asked what "**Mindfulness**" was. She had heard about it but didn't have a clear understanding of how to apply it.

Sometimes it is easier to learn about something by figuring out what it isn't. So, I shared with her how I learned what it is *not*...the hard way.

It was a rainy winter night in Seattle, and I was driving home from work.

The year was 2004.

We had moved our offices the weekend before, so I was mentally and physically exhausted. I also struggle with seasonal allergies, so by the end of the workday, I was starting to feel a headache and congestion.

I thought that I would go home and rest after my last patient, but I had to stop at the grocery store. While at the store, I felt a little dizzy, so I decided to stop shopping, check out what few items I had in the cart, and go home.

While driving home, my mind wandered. I started thinking about the next day. It was my birthday, and I had taken the day off. I was wondering what I would like to do...drive to the nearby lake, and stop and read a book there, or soak in a lavender bubble bath at home.

Suddenly, I heard a loud crash, saw flashes of light, and felt a big jolt. My airbag inflated. I had been in an accident.

My last memory was going down a narrow lane with houses on both sides. As I came to my senses, someone from the neighborhood was asking me how I was. I asked him what happened. He told me that someone had hit me and my car had spun around. He said that I was lucky my car stopped when it hit the pile of rocks on the lawn of a house.

Apparently, I had zoned out and did not stop at a stop sign. The car coming fast on the crossroad had hit me. A witness had already called the police, and they were on their way. I could see my right hand on the steering wheel, and it was crooked.

I will share the remainder of this story later, but for now, the question is...Why did I get into that accident?

It was because **my mind was not present in the moment**. It was wandering somewhere else. I was not mindful.

I learned that when I am not fully present in the moment, I am not mindful. When I am fully present in the moment and experiencing whatever is happening as is, when I am not thinking about the past or the future and not passing judgments, I am mindful.

It is simply a state of present-mindedness or "mind in the moment" without judgments.

Sometimes, this word "mindful" causes some confusion because it sounds similar to "mind full." When I asked my teenage son what the word mindful meant to him, he made a joke about it.

He said, "Mind full means that your mind's computer memory is so full that there is no more space left."

The word "mindful" is quite the opposite. The dictionary definition of mindful is "being conscious or aware of something."

When you are attentive, aware, or careful of something, you are mindful (i.e., mindful of your responsibilities or mindful of other people's needs).

When we use the word psychologically, it refers to a technique whereby you **train your brain** to become more present-minded.

When your thoughts are not going to ten thousand other things, and when you are experiencing what is happening at the moment, you become mindful.

When you are present-minded—besides avoiding accidents—you can feel more relaxed, and you can enjoy your life. You can focus better and become more productive.

When your mind is present, you can think clearly and solve any problems that come your way.

Being mindful also helps to lower your blood pressure and your body's inflammatory reactions, thus improving many health conditions.
You may ask, "If it is good for us, why do people have difficulty staying mindful?"

There are a few reasons for not being able to stay mindful.

Most people can focus on a specific task or project when it is unique, challenging, or novel, but their minds start wandering when they are doing something that is routine.

Do you ever notice that you arrive at a destination and have no recollection of the path you took or what beautiful scenes you passed, especially when you are driving on familiar routes?

Your mind tends to go on autopilot.

A mechanism that was initially meant to help you decrease the work, stops helping when used without awareness.

Instead of staying focused on the task of driving, your mind starts rewinding and reviewing the mental videos of past events or imagining future events, which is what happened when I got into that accident.

This wandering mind is natural, and scientists call it default thinking (I call Mindlessness). In this default thinking mode, your thoughts are automatic, undirected, and superficial.

These thoughts are sometimes useful, but they are generally irrelevant to what you are doing at the moment.

You are looking outside, but not paying attention to anything. Most people spend half their lives in this default thinking mode. It is not necessarily bad...the problem is how much time they spend in that mode versus the time they spend in a focused, sensing mode.

One of my friends said that she is always thinking, even when observing. She has a tendency to observe all the things that are going wrong and that causes more problems for her.

If mindfulness is helpful and if it is thinking about what is around you, why is it causing a problem for her? Is she practicing mindfulness? No.

Mindfulness is not thinking or finding faults in everything. Mindfulness is experiencing the moment.

Although thinking and experiencing are occurring together, becoming aware and giving attention to your experience, including your thoughts, without judgment, is mindfulness.

Let's take the example of observing a sunset.

Scenario One: You are sensing (seeing), appreciating the colors, and enjoying the experience. The thoughts are still there about the colors and how much you are appreciating them, but they are not dominant.

They are in the background. You are aware of them, but your focus is mostly on the experience of the sunset.

Scenario Two: You notice the sunset and the very next moment you start thinking about it, judging, or comparing it to some other experience you had in the past. Or, you start thinking about something different.

Before you know it, the sun is gone and the moment has passed.

You missed enjoying the experience because you were lost in your thoughts.
You were not mindful. What happened?

Although in Scenario One you had some thoughts in the background, you were staying in the moment and experiencing more.

In Scenario Two, your thoughts took over, and the experience went into the background. The more you focus on appreciating the experience no matter how good or bad it feels, the more mindful you are.

You may have noticed that when you are experiencing more and thinking less, you can enjoy life more fully.

To help Sam learn to be mindful while driving, I shared the following instruction with her:

Mindful Driving
When you are mentally present in the process of driving, you are driving mindfully. The next time you are driving somewhere, start with an intention to drive with full presence of mind and to enjoy the process.

As you approach the car, notice the car, its color, its shape, etc.

When you open the door, notice your hand opening the door. As you sit down, notice how the seat feels. As you turn on the ignition, feel your hand moving, and hear the sound of the car starting. Appreciate all of the coordinated movements of your body parts, and feel the sensation of the car moving.

While you are driving, even when you are stuck in traffic, bring attention to your body and observe how your feet smoothly move between the accelerator and the brake pedal.

Observe how your body is automatically breathing.

Look around, see the colors of the cars, the shapes, the roads, the signs, the clouds, the birds, the behavior of other drivers, the trees (or absence of trees), and the perspectives that change moment by moment as the car moves.

Observe the buildings or houses as if you are on a vacation in an unfamiliar place.

When you are stuck in traffic and think, "I am stuck, and I hate it," shift your thoughts to, "It's okay...I can't make the traffic move, but I can observe and enjoy being at the moment." It will make a huge difference in how you feel.

A few weeks later, when I met Sam again, she thanked me for sharing that technique. She told me that every time she got stuck in traffic (which is almost every day), she observed her outside surroundings and her thoughts.

When she started to get "hurry" thoughts, she would tell herself, "There is no sense in punishing myself. I am doing what I can, and I will deal with other issues when I get to work." Although she still had the same commute, she was not stressing as much.

She started to feel **calm.**

Rene
Rene needed to go for a surgical procedure. She was feeling so much stress that her breathing was shallow and her heartbeat was fast. Her blood pressure was so high that the surgeon had to postpone her procedure.

When she talked to me, I reminded her of belly breathing. She took a deep breath and decided to try a meditation, which we had discussed in the past. After a few days, she said, "Meditation is wonderful.

Why didn't I try it before?" She told me that it made her feel calm. She was not feeling as afraid. She was less reactive, got new ideas, and was able to see the positive side in whatever happened.

By practicing meditation, she was able to get her heart rate and her blood pressure back to normal and was able to get her procedure done.

Some people get turned off by the word meditation. They think it is only a religious practice. Although different religions have practiced it for millions of years, it has also been researched for its health benefits.

What is "**Meditation?**" It is simply directing focus. Like a lens merges light energy to a single point, meditation merges your mental energy to one focus. How does it help to train the brain?

Scientifically speaking, your brain's alarm system, the amygdala, becomes enlarged when it gets alarmed signals due to stress. When you meditate, the amygdala gets a break from stress signals. It gets more calm signals, starts shrinking back to normal, and gradually stops causing a severe reaction to every small thing.

How does one meditate?
To meditate, you need a focus that works like an anchor for your floating thoughts. Different types of meditations use different anchors. You can choose any anchor that works for you.

Rene initially chose her breath as an anchor and later added a word that she repeated with every breath. If you want to do it, pick a small (1-2 syllable) word from your value systems like love or peace or relax. Sit with an upright posture. Bring attention to your tummy. Observe how it moves with each breath.

Don't make yourself breathe faster or slower, deeper or shallower…just observe. Let go of the tension in your shoulders and soften your expressions by bringing a slight smile to your face.

Start repeating your word with each breath. Don't do this loudly, or even with tongue, just in your heart. As your mind starts going to other places, keep bringing it back. Even if it gets distracted 1,000 times, bring it back 1,000 times.

You are training your mind, which is like a monkey. It keeps jumping from one branch to another.
With the anchor (word, breath or something else) you are giving it a focus. You are training it.

Each time you bring your attention back, it is like doing a push-up. Each push-up builds your muscles. Similarly, each repetition builds your mental muscle.

Rene started practicing meditation for 5 minutes, 3 times a day, before or after each meal, and later increased her time to 15 minutes, twice a day (in the morning after waking and at night before going to sleep). She started to feel **calm.**

Natasha

Natasha had other issues. Her work was so all-encompassing that she said, "Rozina, I know about meditation, but I don't have any time." She explained, "My day starts frantically, and then I get so busy with the day's work that I don't remember. How can I solve this problem?"

I realized that I also frequently get trapped in a similar time cage. I started searching for something that would help. How do I solve this problem? **"I Don't Have Time" and "I Forget."**

What worked for her was one of the relaxation exercises that she could do while transitioning from one place to another (or one activity to another) called Feet to Floor.

It combines the power of mindfulness, breath work, and muscle relaxation.

Feet to Floor
You can also do Feet to Floor meditation if you don't have a lot of time. It is a very powerful technique, for a few reasons.

First, it only takes one minute. If you tell yourself, "I am going to practice this exercise for only one minute" your mind will say, "Okay, I can do it. I can spare one minute for my health and happiness."

Second, this exercise is associated with transition times. Therefore, it creates a hook for your memory. The name "Feet to Floor" gives you an image of your feet touching the floor. (You can keep a picture of this image in different spots).

When you put your feet on the floor when getting off of your bed, out of your chair, your car, or your house, it can remind you to do this exercise.

This exercise has three simple steps:

1. Feel the body
2. Release the tension
3. Observe the surroundings

1. Feel the body

As your feet touch the floor, take a deep breath and feel them on the ground. How does that touch feel? Do you feel your slippers or shoes or the floor directly? Is the floor hard or soft? Is the feeling comfortable or painful?

You can wiggle or move your feet if needed. If you feel any tension, release it.

Move your attention from your feet to your calves. Are your clothes touching your calves? Are your calves tense or relaxed? If they're relaxed, enjoy. If they're tense, relax and move your attention to your thighs.

Are your thigh muscles feeling tense or relaxed? If they're relaxed, enjoy. If they're tense then relax and notice the difference.

Next, move your attention to your hips. Are your hips tense or relaxed? If they're relaxed then enjoy. If they're tense then relax and feel the difference.

Next, move your attention to your back. Are your back muscles tense or relaxed? If they're relaxed, enjoy. If they're tense, relax and notice the difference.

Next, move your attention to your abdomen.

Is your abdomen feeling tense or relaxed? If it's relaxed, enjoy. If it's tense, then relax and notice the difference. You may also notice if your stomach feels hungry or full. You don't have to stop exercise and run to eat something right away. Just observe at this time.

Next, move your attention to your chest. Is your chest moving with your breathing? Does it feel tense or relaxed? If it's relaxed, enjoy. If it's tense then relax and notice the difference.

Next, move your attention to your shoulders. Are your shoulders hunched up and tense or down and relaxed? If they're relaxed, enjoy. If they're tense, relax and move your attention to your arms.

Are your arms tense or relaxed? If they're relaxed, enjoy. If they're tense, relax and move your attention to your hands.

Make fists with your hands. Feel the tension, relax, and notice the difference.

Next, move your attention to your jaw.

Is your jaw tense or relaxed? If it's relaxed, enjoy. If it's tense, relax and move your attention to your face.

Are your facial muscles tense or relaxed? If they're relaxed, enjoy. If they're tense, relax. Notice the difference and take a relaxing breath.

2. Release the Tension

Next, take a deep breath in, hold for few seconds and tense your whole body from head to toe, as if you are a big wooden log. Breathe out with a forceful "aah"! As you let go of the breath, feel the tension go from your head, through your body, to the earth below your feet, and relax your whole body.

3. Observe your Surroundings

Now open your eyes and look around. Notice everything as if you are seeing things for the first time—shapes, colors, things, and space within which everything exists. As if you are adjusting the focus on a camera, clear your perspective and take a panoramic view. Take a snapshot in your mind's eye.

Focus on hearing what you hear (e.g., sounds of traffic, people talking, wind blowing, or machines humming). Also, appreciate the sounds of your breathing and the silence within which all the noises exist.

Feel the sensation on your skin. Observe your posture. Smell the things you can smell and feel the taste in your mouth. Is your mouth dry or wet? Observe your breathing; is it fast or slow, deep or shallow?

What are your emotions at this moment, and what are the thoughts going through your mind? If the thoughts you have at this particular time are only related to this exercise, then you have achieved your goal: to be thoroughly and deeply mindful in the moment.

If your mind is filled with many thoughts, accept that as well.

The goal of the exercise is to learn to observe. By quieting your mind, you can come to the present moment and become aware of both your external and internal environments.

Become completely aware of the moment and release everything with a deep breath. Feel gratitude in your heart, bring a smile to your face, and go on to your next activity.

Just remember to keep the presence of mind.

It might take more than a minute to learn, but once you do, it will take less than a minute to practice. If you practice each time you transition between activities, you will get this calming benefit several times a day.

Before your stress increases, you will break the cycle, so your stress will remain manageable. If you take these regular breaks, you will feel more alive, attentive, and relaxed. Your focus will improve, your joy will increase, and your stress will drift away.

Active Meditation
In addition to mindfulness with activities and one-minute meditations, there is also the reward of quieting the brain for longer periods of time with formal meditation.

There are many health benefits of meditation and doctors are prescribing it as a way of calming the body and decreasing blood pressure, inflammation, IBS, migraine, chronic pain, and many stress-related conditions.

I also prescribe it.

Some of my patients have a hard time practicing due to their active minds. Our active minds are similar to monkeys, restlessly jumping all the time.

You cannot expect a monkey to stop jumping unless it engages in some other activity. If it gets focused on the new activity, it will and stop jumping...at least for a short time.

Like many people, it has been hard for me to meditate sometimes. Spiritual meditation is a part of my faith practice, so I try to meditate.

I find that my mind is always traveling in many directions. Sometimes, I even use an alarm, which I keep snoozing, so it continually brings my attention back to center.

When it goes off, I realize that I was either thinking of something else or falling asleep in odd positions.

Sometimes I just open my journal and start writing. It settles my jumpy thoughts.

In the past, whenever I used to write during my meditation time, I would feel guilty. One time, I was sharing my dilemma with my colleague Dr. Berger, who has many years of mindful meditation practice.

I confessed that sometimes I am not able to sit, "do nothing," and "just be," and that I feel guilty for writing in my journal. I told him that I get my best ideas when I write and I get absorbed. It calms me. It excites me.

His comment dissolved my feelings of guilt. He said, "Rozina, recognize that writing is your meditation."

I had my "aha moment." **Writing could be meditation too!**

If you have a similar problem, don't despair. Any intentional activity that helps you bring your focus to one point, helps you calm down, and helps you develop reflective thinking, is your meditation.

If your mind is not ready for one of the formal meditations, you can train it by using one of the active meditations (like writing as I did or art as my husband did).

My husband has an electronic engineering degree. He used to work in the corporate world.

Although he doodled as a child and had considered art his preferred career choice while growing up, he had given up that desire after family members and career counselors had advised him to do something that would make him money, and practice art "on the side."

As a result, he did not touch art for roughly 20 years of his adult life.

Then, when he was going through stressful times at work, he started painting again to relieve the stress. Sometimes he would paint at night when he couldn't sleep, and I would wake up to a beautiful painting!
Not only did painting help him relax, but it also inspired him to think outside of the box. It gave him the courage to change his field and follow his passion.

Today, he has an art studio where he teaches art, creates his artwork, and is pursuing an advanced degree in art education.

When I noticed how inspired, energized, and engrossed he gets when he is doing his art, I started a workshop with him called "Create, Relax, and Heal."

I have seen participants get so absorbed in the art that they seem to forget all of their worries. They quiet their minds of all their stressful thoughts. Therefore, I call this form of expression **Art Meditation**.

Any form of art can be meditative: music, dance, drawing, and painting.

Even the simple act of coloring is so meditative that 3 of the 10 bestselling books of 2015 were adult coloring books, and today most bookstores have a section entirely dedicated to adult coloring.

When you do something with full presence of mind, it provides both relaxation and a space for reflection that leads to positive energy, joy, health, and peace.

Many people find art very meditative due to its intrinsic ability to provide a calm space and focus, which can also heal many stress-related illnesses.

I witnessed the healing power of art during my psychiatry residency at UIC around 1997.

I had a patient assigned to me for psychotherapy who had developed PTSD (Post Traumatic Stress Disorder) from his Vietnam War experience. In therapy, he had a very hard time talking about his feelings related to his trauma, but he needed frequent hospitalization due to flashbacks.

His flashbacks were so bad that he used to scream his fellow soldiers' names and hide behind things.
As we explored different ways for him to express himself, we talked about how different colors can convey different moods.

He had never touched a brush in his life, so he was initially reluctant to try articulating his thoughts through colors.

Nevertheless, he started revealing his feelings in painting.

At the VA hospital, paint and paper were usually available to patients. He regularly began picking up the brush and making different color strokes after his group therapy.

When he brought those paintings to me, he was able to share how he felt at that time. It allowed him to process and let go of his distressed feelings. Slowly, he started to calm down.

His hospitalization rate decreased.

When I announced that I was leaving the clinic after my graduation, he wanted to give me the gift of some of his paintings.

I advised that I could not take any gift of significant monetary value, but I would accept a card. In response, he made a card-size wood carving of a water lily in a pond by a palm tree that said, "This represents peace inside me."

That was the best evidence I've seen of the calming power of art.

In this chapter, I offered several calming techniques and you can choose what works best for you.

Once Sam, Rene, and Natasha acknowledged that stress was taking a toll on them, they picked a calming technique that aligned with their personalities or lifestyles to help reduce stress and anxiety.

What are you doing to calm your mind and body?

If you're doing nothing, pick one of the aforementioned ways and start practicing. You may know many techniques, but knowing is not enough.

You need to also practice. No matter how much you know about a mango, you won't be able to experience the taste or benefit from its nutrition unless you eat it.

Similarly, no matter how many different techniques you research, unless you incorporate these relaxation practices, you cannot feel the calming effect on your mind and body.

In each of my friends' cases, they knew many ways to relax and calm down; but it only helped them when they started practicing.

I suggest you also pick one of the exercises and start your practice today.

Many people only try to practice relaxation when they are most distressed. If you do that, it would be like only practicing on game day.

With the high pressure of competition, your body wouldn't be able to perform well unless you practiced regularly. The same goes for any mental skill. You need to train your brain.

Therefore, I suggest that you pick a time and practice regularly. Somedays you will be able to focus better than others.

Gradually, your mind will learn the skill and will be able to remain calm, even at the most stressful times.

Another thing to watch out for is the trap of "later." One time, I asked a friend who was sharing a saga about work and kids and going through remodeling of her house, "What are you doing to relax?" She said, "I will relax when all this is over."

Do you hear yourself say that sometimes? "I will relax when all this is over." Is "this" ever going to be all over?

After "this," there will be another "this." You will always find yourself waiting for something else to be over before you relax. Life is never going to be "all over" until it is the end, and then it will be too late.

Life is like a bubble of water, and there is no guarantee that it will be here tomorrow. When tomorrow comes, it becomes today. Therefore, "tomorrow never comes."

So, if you want to calm your body and start transforming your stress, pick any exercise and start practicing today.

Take a break, and meditate.

If you don't, you will continue to feel stressed and even simple things will irritate you. If you do, you will be able to break the stress cycle and prevent it from reaching the tipping point.

As you calm your mind, you will be ready for the next step on your journey from stress to joy. In the next chapter, let's explore the step represented by **R** in the acronym **ACR** for the basic steps of the journey from stress to joy.

Chapter 3

Reflect:

How to use effective tools to think through your issues and solutions.

You have calmed down your mind and body with mindfulness, meditation, and other relaxation exercises. Now what? Your problems have not completely resolved.

The problems that were caused by a tense body and overwhelmed mind are starting to decrease, yet you still need to take further steps to resolve your problem.

Your clear mind can now help you focus on possible solutions instead of feeling overwhelmed by the problems.

Before calming down, your mind was so overwhelmed with emotions that it was hard to think logically.

As your mind settles, you can reflect on your situation. In this chapter, let's review some tools and techniques to help you do that.

Sam
As Sam calmed her frustration by practicing mindful driving, her mind cleared. So, she started reflecting on her situation and brainstorming her options with friends and family.

Rene
As Rene calmed down, she began listing all of the stuff she had to do, so she could reflect on her priorities.

Natasha
As Natasha calmed her mind and body, she reflected on what was working for her that she wanted to continue and what was not working for her that she wanted to change.

As they started to calm their minds and bodies, these women were able to reflect on their situations. The third step in this transformative journey from stress to joy is to **Reflect**—represented by **R** in the acronym **ACR.**

The skill of reflective thinking is what allows someone to change an unhealthy reaction to a healthy response.

Now you may be questioning, "Don't reaction and response mean the same thing?"

Yes and no. Although both refer to how you face a certain situation, in psychological terms, they are different due to how they affect you. A "reaction" is addressing a particular situation without awareness, just as a knee-jerk happens automatically.

81

But a "response" is responding to the situation with intention. The difference is that your knee-jerk reaction can lead to ill health whereas the thought-out response can lead to health.

Let's try to understand it further.

If you review your successes in the past, you will notice that in most cases, you had reflected on your situation.

You recognized your problem.

You realized what was working and what was not and then intentionally decided to respond by making changes that resulted in your success.

Similarly, when you develop a habit of reflecting on your situation and possible solutions, you will successfully transform your stress.

Until you develop this skill of reflective thinking, you are likely to react to many situations without thinking, like one of my patients. I'll call him John.

John used to get very angry while driving, especially when someone crossed him in traffic.

One day when this happened during the morning rush, he got so upset that he followed the other driver.

As soon as he got a chance, he blocked the other car. He got out and started screaming at the other driver to get out of the car.
The other driver promptly rolled up his window when he saw John approaching and called 911.

John got so angry that he started punching the other car and made a few dents before the police arrived at the scene.

What was the result? **A $700 ticket.**

Later in court, the judge asked him what he was thinking when he was banging on that car with his fists. John realized that he was not consciously thinking about anything!

He was just reacting, without awareness.

Do you ever react without thinking and do something that you regret later? Do you want to avoid reacting like that and start responding with intention?

You may have noticed that as you continue the practice of mindfulness, you are also preparing to be able to reflect. What can you do to further develop this reflective thinking skill?

Let's see what helped some of our friends.

Sam
As Sam was calming down with her mindful driving, her awareness increased. She noticed that her thoughts tended to keep repeating and going back and forth.

She was used to writing things down to organize her thoughts about her work projects. She decided to do that for her growth project as well.

She realized that she was able to come up with great advice when her friends or colleagues came to her to brainstorm, but it was hard to come up with advice for herself.

Therefore, when I shared with her one journaling technique I use, she was able to relate, employ the practice, and benefit.

I shared how I came to using it when I was feeling helpless, stuck and overwhelmed with various demands in my life.

I call this technique the "**Self-Dialogue Journal.**"

A few years ago, I had a realization while talking to one of my patients, who was a nurse by profession.

One day, she was sharing how she was feeling stuck and overwhelmed due to multiple demands in her life. She was not able to find time for her self-care.

We brainstormed options. She kept on saying, "Yes, but I can't do that because—" Finally, we identified a few solutions that could work for her.

After the session, I realized that I was going through the same stuck feeling. My back hurt, and I knew that going for a chiropractic adjustment could help me, as it had in the past.

I just could not find the time to schedule an appointment. Like many caretakers, I felt guilty when I had to cancel my patients' appointments to take care of myself on a workday.

I realized that I am a great adviser when it comes to others. I could brainstorm so many ways that my patient could make time to take care of herself, but I was not able to see those options for myself.

I got an idea and decided to help myself.

The following weekend, I opened my journal and started writing a dialogue between a patient and a doctor where I was both the patient and the doctor. I focused on the **issue**, the **options**, and the best action **plan** (IOP).

I was complaining about how I felt helpless and stuck in a web of my own creation (the way I had scheduled my life). Whenever I came up with a suggestion, my mind kept repeating the argument, "Yes, but I can't do that because…"

I wrote for an hour and a half that day, and finally, a plausible solution popped up in my writing that had not come to my mind before.

At that time, I used to work Monday through Friday, 9am-5pm with a one-hour break for lunch.

But what if I could change one Friday per month to 9am-2pm, without a lunch break, freeing up three hours for personal appointments?

At that time, my financial situation did not allow me to take a full day off, but I *could* decrease my patient scheduling by two hours per month.

That was plausible.

Once I reached that option, I said aloud to myself, "Now follow your advice."

Although I was not able to implement the change for another month (as my schedule mostly gets booked weeks to months in advance), I still felt immediate relief since I felt that *I could do something* about the situation.

I felt like a big burden was lifted from my shoulders. I was no longer a helpless victim. I was an empowered victor.

Since I first did this exercise to help myself several years ago, I have seen it serve many friends, patients, and seminar attendees.

A teacher used the technique successfully when she wrote the dialogue between a teacher and a student and then followed her advice.

A mother used a mother/daughter dialogue, and a friend used a friend/friend dialogue. You can use whatever works for you to see the power of stepping out of your way.

I think the reason this exercise works so well is that you get out of your victim role and become the helper or well-wisher for yourself. It is hard to think about solutions when you are so entrenched in the role of a victim.

You are usually much kinder to someone else than you are to yourself. When you write like this and step out of your role, your inner wisdom comes out, and you can take on the victor role.

You can download an example dialogue for the Self Dialogue Journal at http://stresstojoy.com/resources.

Rene

As Rene started reflecting, she noticed that her thinking was mostly focused on what was not working.

It was making her feel overwhelmed and guilty.

To help her shift her focus to what was working in her life, I shared a simple form of journaling called a **Gratitude Journal**, which I teach to most of my patients. She started writing ten things for which she felt grateful, every morning.

She noticed that her focus was shifting from what was missing in her life to what was working.

As I teach this technique, sometimes it is hard for people to get into the habit of doing something they are not used to, especially when they are hurting.

I tell them, if you don't feel ready yet, that is okay. It is very hard when you are in pain because all of your attention goes to your pain. Listen to your body.

Acknowledge how you feel and calm down with meditation and mindfulness. As you start reflecting, at some point you will be ready to ask yourself, "When am I willing to stop feeling this miserable?"

If your answer is **now**, then you are ready.

Although you may be contemplating for a long time, the decision to change happens in an instant. How do I know this? I know because I have gone through it myself.

Let me share how I first started my Gratitude Journal.
As I mentioned earlier, the years after my car accident in 2004 were incredibly challenging.

I had crushed the small bone under the thumb of my right wrist. It was so bad that the surgeon had to put 10 screws in that bone just to stabilize it.

The pain and swelling were so severe that I couldn't do the simple tasks of daily living like opening a food jar, dialing a phone, or even zipping my pants.

I had to ask a friend to get a few pairs of pants with elastic tops for me, so I didn't have to zip.

My husband had to open jars of food before he left for work, so I could eat. The hardest thing was that suddenly I could not properly take care of my five-year-old son.

My husband had to take over, helping him with daily showers and getting him ready for school. I felt helpless, guilty, and depressed. I was crying a lot and feeling sorry for myself.

After a few weeks, my husband took me to see some out-of-town relatives for a change of environment.

One day during the visit, my relative helped me get in the shower. She asked me to call her when I was finished since I was not able to put on clothes by myself.

She left me in the shower upstairs and went downstairs for a few minutes to join in the family discussion.

It had been a long time since the last family gathering, so she got busy talking and laughing at the dining table.

When I was finished showering, I called out but she couldn't hear me above the noise. I called a few times, but no one came up for some time. I felt incredibly helpless.

Imagine how you would feel if you were finished showering but weren't able to leave the bathroom because you couldn't put on your clothes without help. I went back into the shower stall and started crying, almost screaming. I started banging the shower wall with my left hand.

Suddenly, I had an epiphany: I am hitting the shower wall with my left hand! What if I had lost both of my hands? What if I had lost my mind, my life, or my child?

A feeling of gratitude surged through me. At least I had my left hand. I felt an instant change in my attitude.

I remembered Dr. Kabat-Zinn's words from his book *Full Catastrophe Living*: "As long as you are breathing, there is more right with you than wrong."

After that day, I stopped crying all the time. I ceased to feel sorry for myself as much.

I developed a different appreciation for life.

The new feeling was strong for a few days, but its level fluctuated. What helped make it more sustainable was *the gratitude journal.*

I can still vividly see the first day when I started my gratitude journal. It was about a month after the accident, and I just couldn't sleep. I am a right-sided sleeper, and the stabilizing screws on my right hand prohibited me from lying on my preferred side.

I sat up that night and noticed a journal that my friend Gloria had gifted to me.

I picked it up with my left hand, picked up a pen, and started scribbling with my left hand— I had never written with my left hand before that night. In my crooked handwriting, I wrote, *"I am grateful for being able to write with my left hand."*

I knew that I wanted to focus on positives but found it hard to do that when I was in so much pain.

I was only able to write a few other things that night—with the capacity to endure the pain, a pillow to rest my hands, eyes to see beyond my window, and a husband sleeping by my side.

Since that day, I have written in my gratitude journal almost every day and I teach it to most of my patients.

When I am writing prescriptions for them toward the end of the session, I usually ask them, "Tell me three things you are most grateful for." Then I ask them to write those in their gratitude journal daily.

When I surveyed my patients, they told me that journaling was the most helpful technique they had learned from me.

It helped them shift their focus to what was working and set a positive tone for the day.

You can download an example and template for the Gratitude Journal from http://stresstojoy.com/resources

IGF

If you want to start your practice, all you have to do is get a journal or a notebook, keep it by your bedside, or carry it in your purse. Write in it before you start your busy day. It could be a few simple lines starting with the prompt:

"Today **I** am **G**rateful **F**or..." (or **IGF** for short) and write down whatever comes to your mind. These could be simple things like, "I am grateful for my eyes so I can see" or "I am grateful for my hands so I can hold things."

They could also be abstract things like, "I am grateful for the love, peace, and security." You may repeat things or write different things each day.

If you have difficulty coming up with things to be grateful for, one way that helps is to ask, "What are the ordinary things that are working to make today happen? What are the things that I may have taken for granted?

What will I miss if it is not there?" If you still have difficulty, look toward others who may not have simple life necessities like water or electricity or eyesight.

With natural disasters and man-made tragedies, you will find plenty of things that people only miss when they lose them. You will start appreciating the *extraordinariness of ordinary.*

Will you miss your eyes? Will you miss your ability to breathe, smell, taste, touch, stand, walk, or talk?
Will you miss your family?
Will you miss your home? Will you miss your job?

Although family, home, and job are the most common things people identify, one lady identified her legs so she could go to the bathroom by herself.

I was intrigued and asked her why, since that is not a common thing people identify. She said she works as a caretaker and provides assistance for people who are bedridden. She realizes how important it is to have legs so you can go to the bathroom without help.

Do you take any of these for granted?

What are you grateful for today?

If you have a *general* attitude of gratitude in your heart, that is great. Continue.

What I have found, however, is that when you have a habit of saying, "Thank God for everything," sometimes it becomes rote.

You may not feel the deep gratitude even though you may be saying it with the tongue.

When you have gratitude for *specific* things in addition to giving general thanks, it invites you to think more deeply and appreciate what you may take for granted otherwise.

Some people don't like to write about their gratitude. They just think about it. If you are like that, continue to think and feel grateful.

I have found that it is easier to think positive thoughts when things are going well, but it is harder when things are not going so smoothly.

If you have a routine like writing a gratitude journal daily, it will help you maintain that attitude of gratitude, even in hard times.

Some people use a rosary, and some people carry rocks or other tokens in their pockets to remind them.
These are all helpful tools, and I encourage you to use whatever works for you.

For many of the people with whom I have shared this technique, writing deepens the feeling of gratitude and establishes the habit most effectively.

You may ask, "What is the best time to write?" For me, writing about my gratitude first thing in the morning works best as it sets the tone for the whole day. For some people (like Oprah Winfrey), writing at night works better.

Do whatever works for you.

If you find it hard to write in the morning or the evening, find hidden pockets of time during your busy day (waiting at a doctor's office, between meetings at work or on lunch break).

Carry your diary/journal with you, and write when you find these pockets of otherwise wasted time.

Natasha
When Natasha was having some difficulty reflecting and I suggested writing, she had several reservations, like, "I am afraid someone will read it," or "I don't write well."

"Last time I tried to write, I felt more negative, since it brought out so many negative thoughts."

If you are afraid someone will read it, there's a simple solution. Tear the paper up after writing.

If you are not writing to show anyone, does it matter if you write well? All that matters is that you offload your mind and clear your mental space of mental garbage.

Do you find that you feel more negative when writing because it brings about negative thoughts? That happens to people since they may have kept the negative thoughts suppressed for too long.

Some people initially feel bad, but then feel better after letting out the negative thoughts in the form of writing.

If you are able to bring the negative thoughts out of your mind and let them go, you can clear your mental space. Wouldn't it be better if they were released instead of staying inside of you?

When they stay inside, they get lodged in your body and cause problems.

You don't have to do anything that makes you feel bad.

If bringing those negative thoughts to your consciousness adversely affects you, it may not be the right tool for you, it may not be the right time for you, or you may need additional help working with a therapist before you can use this tool.

Write only if you feel it is right.

Natasha felt it was right for her, so she scheduled a daily 15-minute time slot in her planner. She made a routine of starting a timer and putting her pen on a notepad.

She wrote whatever came to her mind.

As soon as the time was over, she put the pen down, tore the pages of the notepad into small pieces, and threw them into her wastebasket. It felt good to get rid of that garbage.
This technique is called **"Therapeutic Writing."**

Therapeutic writing helps many chronic pain patients get rid of their pain. How is that possible?

When I first heard about it from a spine surgeon in Seattle named Dr. Hanscom, I was intrigued.

I scheduled a meeting with him to learn more. He graciously gave me his time and shared how he uses this technique in a rehab program before his patients get spine surgery.

He said that this technique even helped him when he suffered from chronic pain for more than 13 years. When he got better, he developed a program and wrote a book called *Back in Control.* You can learn more about this program and get a lot of helpful tools from his website: http://backincontrol.com.

Dr. Hanscom told me that about 75% of the people who come to him with the intention of having surgery for their back pain end up not needing the surgery when they participate in this program, where therapeutic writing is one of the major techniques.

When I talked to him in 2016, he said that more than 800 people were able to get rid of their chronic back pain without surgery using this program.

Amazing!

Why do you think this technique helps so many people with chronic pain? I think that many people carry a lot of anger and hurt in their bodies.

Writing the thoughts down is like clearing the mind's space from rotting garbage. Putting the thoughts on paper tells the mind that those thoughts are just thoughts, not you.

They are separate from you. Most of all, the act of tearing and ritualistically throwing away the paper tells the mind that you can get rid of those negative thoughts.

The bonus is that by throwing the paper away, you don't have to worry about someone reading it!

What do you do when the clutter builds up in your house, and things start to smell? You do a major cleanup and then develop some regular habits to keep the area clean and organized, right?

Similarly, you need to empty your mind's bin of negative thoughts, clear your mental space of unnecessary worries, and regularly organize your thoughts.

Journaling helps you effectively do that. Journaling helps you develop reflective thinking. I have come to appreciate my journal so much that I'd call it my best friend.

You may be wondering; how can a journal be a
friend?
Do you have friends who help you by listening
to you?

Friends are great sources of joy and happiness
for many.
They make handling stress easier. How? What
do best friends do?
Think about it for a minute.
They take care of each other.
They are emotionally supportive.
They are there when you need them.
They listen and uplift.
They bring you out of the dumps.
They alleviate loneliness.
They share resources.
They share their deepest feelings.
They cry with you, laugh with you, go places
with you, and give you feedback.

Having a friend provides you with love, a sense
of belonging, and a feeling of being cared for.

Now if you review your list of friends, most of
them meet *some* of these criteria, but someone
rarely meets *all* of the criteria.

But who is the friend who can meet all of the
criteria and is with you all of the time?

The answer is *you*.

You are in constant communication with yourself in the form of self-talk. You may notice that your self-talk is your best friend or your worst enemy. It can help you feel enlivened if it's positive or make you feel worse if it's negative. You can train your brain to produce self-talk that lifts you up instead of depressing you.

Some people process things in their brains. Processing always happens in the brain's computer, but downloading it on an external drive allows space in the hard drive for better organization and efficient processing.

I download my thoughts into my journal. I use my journal to communicate with my "self."

I have found that I get feedback from my inner self in my writing.
When I list the pros and cons of my options, it helps me to make decisions, and it usually helps me organize my priorities. In that way, my journal is my friend.

As I mentioned earlier, reflection always happens internally. Writing it down brings it to your consciousness, clarifies the message, and helps you listen to yourself.

The brain tends to repeatedly bring up an issue because it is afraid that you will forget. When you write it down, your brain relaxes because it thinks that you won't.

As Sam, Rene, and Natasha reflected, they went through a series of steps in the process. I saw a pattern in the steps they went through and developed a formula that you can apply to any stressful situation.

Would you like to learn that formula? For the ease of learning, let's look at each component of this formula individually in the next few chapters.

Chapter 4
Recognize:

How to stop wasting time on something you can't control.

Do you pick up the pen to start reflecting and journaling and then feel writer's block? Do you desire a system of writing that would help you to reflect in any stressful situation?

Usually, formulas help to replicate a process. The formula for reflection that can help you on your journey from stress to joy is **3R with CPR**.

3R represents three steps of reflection, and CPR represents three ways of strengthening your chosen response.

You will notice that although these reflections are happening simultaneously in your mind, it makes it easier to master the process when you learn each component separately.

In this chapter, let's learn the first R of the formula 3R with CPR through the example of our three friends.

Sam
A few days after we had talked about the mindful driving, Sam told me that she was reflecting on her situation and had her "aha moment."

She **recognized** that although her employer's expectations were causing some stress, the way she was reacting to those demands was adding to her stress.

Her work and commute demands were not in her control, but the way she was giving higher priority to her work than to other aspects of her life was in her control.

She recognized that she was feeling overwhelmed because she was spending 60-65 hours per week at work and commuting (which was the external stressor not in her control) and she was feeling even more affected because she was thinking about work even when she was not working.

She recognized that when she was not mindful and not making her priorities her choice, her circumstances were choosing for her.

It was becoming her choice by default.

Without intention, she was choosing not to socialize or take care of her body and mind. Due to a lack of awareness, she was not dedicating enough time to spend with her family.

Even when she was with them, her mind was thinking, worrying, or feeling upset about her work.

She recognized that if she got sick, her work was not going to come to her to aid. If she was not able to perform, her employer would replace her, but her body would have to deal with the consequences.

She recognized that her body, her mind, and her family were her biggest assets, and she needed to take care of her assets.

Rene
As Rene started reflecting, she **recognized** that the client demands were coming from outside of her circle of control, but how she was prioritizing her tasks was inside her circle.

She recognized that she was giving more importance to her client's needs than her own.

She was self-sabotaging by getting irritable with her family. That led to feeling guilty, emotional eating, weight gain, and ultimately more guilt. She was stuck in the stress cycle.

> She recognized that to continue or change was her choice.

Natasha
As Natasha started reflecting, she recognized that although one of her coworkers was mean and demanding, her own passive-aggressive reaction was adding to her stress level.

She recognized that her constant worrying was keeping her mind so active that she could not sleep.

When she was not able to sleep, her frustration level got so high that even a small comment by a coworker was agitating.

She could not control her coworker's behavior, but she could influence the situation in some ways by the way she responded (her words, her facial expressions, and her behavior).

She understood the concept of 'the circle of influence,' a term used by Stephen Covey, a leader in leadership literature and author of *The Seven Habits of Highly Effective People*.

What is the **"Circle of Influence?"**

Many times, when my patients are concerned about other people's behavior that they can't do much about, I frequently draw two circles. The outer circle represents everything that concerns you.

Some of those issues are totally out of your control. You can't do anything about them. Some aspects are in your control. You can take *some* action.

These actions form the **inner circle**.

By your actions, you can *influence* issues of your concern in some ways. Therefore, the inner circle is called the circle of influence.

You can write, "I can" inside the inner circle and "Others can" outside this inner circle.

When you focus on things you can do, you feel empowered. When you focus on things you can't do that are outside of your circle, that you expect others to do, you feel frustrated.

Furthermore, when you waste your time and energy focusing on things you can't do anything about, very little of your time and energy is left to focus on things you can do something about.

112

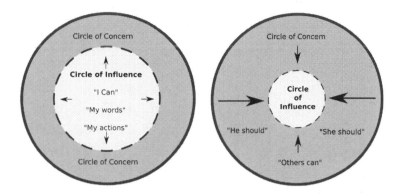

Natasha had an "aha moment" when she
understood, "The more you focus on the issues
inside the circle of influence, the more your
influence increases. When you focus on the
issues outside of your circle of influence, your
influence decreases."

She understood that the more she focused on
trying to change her coworker (which was
outside her circle), the less energy she had left
for changing her behavior (which was inside
her circle) and influencing her team.

"90/10 Principle" made this understanding
stronger. Stephen Covey stated that "10% of
life is made up of what happens to you, and
90% of life is decided by how you react." Think
about that for a moment.

If 90% of your life is how you react to your environment, people, and situations around you, then wouldn't 90% of stress also be due to how you react?

If so, then the things that make you feel stuck, hopeless, and further your stress, even if totally out of your control, are only 10% of life. It also means that you can modify 90% of your stress level by modifying how you react.

It was difficult for me to accept this principle until I read this clear and concise example, and suddenly it made sense.

Let's imagine you are eating breakfast with your family. Your ten-year-old daughter knocks over a cup of coffee onto your business shirt. You have no control over what just happened. What happens next, however, will be determined by how you react.

Scenario 1: You curse. You harshly scold your daughter for knocking over the coffee cup. She breaks down in tears. After scolding her, you turn to your spouse and criticize him or her for placing the cup too close to the edge of the table.
A short verbal battle follows.
You storm upstairs and change your shirt.

Back downstairs, you find your daughter has been too busy trying to finish her breakfast to get ready for school. She misses the bus.
Your spouse must leave immediately for work, so you rush to the car and drive your daughter to school. Already running late, you drive 40 mph in a 30-mph speed zone. You're pulled over by a police officer, who writes you a ticket.

After an additional 15-minute delay (throwing money away on a traffic fine), you finally arrive at the school.
Your daughter runs into the building without saying goodbye.
After arriving at your office 20 minutes late, you find you forgot your briefcase in all of the mayhem.
Your day has started terribly. As it continues, it seems to get worse and worse. You look forward to going home.
When you arrive home, you detect a wedge in your relationship with your spouse and daughter. Why? Why did you have a bad day?

A. Did the coffee cause it?
B. Did your daughter cause it?
C. Did the police officer cause it?
D. Did you cause it?

The answer is D.

You had no control over what happened with the coffee. How you reacted in that split second is what kicked off the stress → reaction → stress cycle and *"caused"* your bad day. That split second is when your automatic thoughts and your habitual emotional reactions kicked in and caused you to behave the way you did.

Scenario 2: The coffee splashes onto your shirt, and you notice your daughter is about to cry. You acknowledge your frustration and the negative internal dialogue. You take a deep breath and calm down.
You reflect and question your negative thoughts. The coffee has spilled for only the second time in ten years since your daughter's birth.
Most of the time your daughter doesn't spill coffee. It was just an accident, and accidents happen. She is a caring kid. She will learn in time.

This way of thinking shifts any negative thoughts into a positive frame. *The cycle breaks!*

With the change in your internal dialogue, your reaction creates a very different start to your day.

Your tone softens as you lean over to your daughter and say, *"It's okay, honey. Let's finish breakfast and be more careful next time."*

These stories indicate that as our friends started reflecting, they had to **Recognize** their role in their stress cycle, focus on things they can do, and pick options that were inside their circle of influence.

Recognize is the first R of the formula 3R with CPR.

As you reflect on your situation, are you able to recognize your role in your stress cycle? Ask yourself if your focus is inside your circle of influence?
You can download a template to jot down issues inside and outside your circle of influence at http://stresstojoy.com/resources

Once you recognize that your reaction is adding to your stress, you'll want to figure out *why* you are reacting in ways that are not helping you. The second R of the 3R formula helps you figure out those reasons. Let's explore how to **Realize** those reasons in the next chapter.

Chapter 5

Realize:

How to determine why you continue to do what doesn't work.

No one intentionally thinks or behaves in a manner that would cause further stress and suffering. If you are reacting in a way that is causing more stress and suffering, then you want to figure out why. In this chapter, let's reflect on those reasons.

Sam
When Sam recognized that she was making choices that were adding to her stress, she asked herself why she was giving more priority to her work over other important aspects of her life.

As she reflected, she identified her underlying automatic thought: if she works like that, she will get promoted to the position of CFO.

She asked herself why she wanted to be the CFO and realized her underlying belief. She believed that the higher position would allow her to make a more substantial difference for others in the world.

Looking at the bigger picture, she realized that if she feels stressed, she can't make any difference for others.

She explored alternative thoughts that were more in alignment with her value system. She realized that whichever position she was in, she could create a significant impact on her clients and her company by establishing a better balance in her life.

Rene
When Rene thought deeply about why she was reacting by eating, she realized that she did not have a constructive outlet when something frustrated her. She remembered that while growing up, her parents gave her food to feel better every time she had any strong feeling.

That led to an underlying belief that food would make her feel better when she was frustrated. She was still reacting based on this same belief, even though her reality had changed.

Excessive sweet food had a different effect on her as an adult because every time she was eating it, she felt worse. Once she realized that, she was able to explore alternatives.

When she feels overwhelmed with multiple demands, her mind says, "Eat something sweet, and it will make you feel better." She can counter that thought with, "Yes, food may make me feel good for a few minutes, but the guilt and weight gain will ultimately make me feel worse."

She realized that sweet food had become a withdrawal from her emotional coping account instead of a deposit. She knew that she needed another healthy outlet when she felt frustrated.

She liked music and nature, so her alternative thought was: *Music and nature make me feel better both in the short and long term. Let me make a folder of my favorite songs and listen while going for a nature walk.*

She also recognized that the underlying thought causing her to digress and procrastinate was: *There are so many tasks, I can never do them all!* When she changed the thought to: *These are a lot of tasks, but they are still finite in number. I can prioritize and do the most important tasks first*, it made her feel better.

Before changing the thought, she felt her tasks would never end, but changing the thought from "too many tasks" to "a finite number of tasks" made her feel less overwhelmed.

She realized that changing her thoughts can help her change her feelings.

Natasha
When Natasha reflected on why she was feeling so worried and upset, she realized she had a pattern of making things bigger than what they actually were (magnifying). She identified an angry thought she had that a certain coworker was trying to make her lose her job.

She was worried that she was going to lose everything near and dear to her (catastrophizing).
"Crossroad Technique" helped her realize her underlying thoughts and their effect. Let's review how to use this technique.

There is usually a 50% chance that things may go positive and a 50% chance that things may go negative.

You have a choice of focusing on positive or negative.

Let's consider each option.

1. If you worry a lot by focusing on a negative outcome and things go positively, you will have **suffered for no reason.**

2. If you focus on the negative and things go negatively, **you will suffer twice.** The first time you will suffer in your mind and a second time after the event occurs.

3. If you focus on the positive and things go positively, **you can be happy all along.**

4. If you focus on the positive and things go negatively, **you can be mentally strong** enough to deal with whatever happens.

Natasha realized she doesn't know for sure what is going to happen in the future. In any situation, there is always a chance that things go negatively or positively. She was so focused on the negative (losing everything) that her mind didn't even think that the *negative* might not happen.

She was already suffering in her mind from some possible negatives (loss of job and everything near and dear to her), which may or may not happen in the undetermined future.

If things go positively, she will have suffered for no reason, and if the negative consequences do happen, she will suffer again in reality.

In essence, she will suffer twice. She didn't want that.

She also realized that she was assigning more importance to her coworker's behavior than was needed. When she realized her automatic thought was that her coworker has a malicious motive, she could change the thought to an alternative thought that her coworker may be having some issues of his own that are driving him to be so grumpy and mean.

Maybe his wife has been diagnosed with cancer, or he is on the verge of getting a divorce. She realized that she doesn't know what the truth is, but changing her thoughts made her feel differently.

You can download the crossroad technique to post in a prominent place to remind you at http://stresstojoy.com/resources

In these stories, did you notice the next step that makes the second R in the formula 3R with CPR? **Realize.**

When these ladies asked themselves why they were reacting in ways that were not helping them, they **realized** their underlying thoughts and beliefs were leading them to their stress reactions.

They understood the myth that only outside events cause your reaction. In reality, the outside events **trigger your automatic thoughts,** which then lead to your reaction.

These automatic thoughts give meaning to any event in your mind. These thoughts act like mental filters. When you change them, they lead to a different reaction. Once you identify them, you acquire the power to change them.

Because this is such an important part of your stress-to-joy journey, let's further explore it.

I shared the story of one of my patients, John, who had gotten a $700 traffic ticket for blocking another car and banging on the car when someone crossed him in traffic.

In court, the judge asked him what he was thinking when he was banging that car with his fists. John had realized that he was not consciously thinking anything. He was habitually reacting, without awareness.

What do you think? Did the driver that crossed him cause him to say those words, feel that anger, or take the action of following or punching the car?

If so, why doesn't he do the same thing every time someone crosses him in traffic?
Do you ever react without awareness?
Have you noticed that some days everything irritates you and some days you are able to handle frustrations? Why? You are the same person, and the event/trigger is the same, so what is the difference?

The difference is the meaning your mind ascribes to the event at that time.

That meaning comes from your automatic thoughts, attitudes, and beliefs you develop through your value system and past experiences. When you change these thoughts, the meaning changes for you and so does your reaction.

The more you change, the more you train your brain to think desirably. How to do that?

There are many techniques used for training your thoughts.

The most popular techniques are CBT (Cognitive Behavior Therapy) and NLP (Neuro-Linguistic Programming).

I find three column techniques from CBT very useful for reprogramming these thoughts. Cognition pertains to thoughts and behavior pertains to actions.

Therefore, these therapies focus on training both thoughts and actions. Most of the evidence-based cognitive therapies share some basic premises. You will find them beneficial if you read these premises out loud.

Basic Premises of Most Cognitive Therapies

1. The way I feel and behave is not caused by the way others treat me or the events that happen to me.

2. The way I feel is created, controlled, and maintained by the interpretation made by my mind.

3. I learned these interpretations at some point in my life.

4. Anything that is learned can be unlearned.

5. I can learn something new.

6. I can change the way I think (interpret).

7. When I change the way I interpret, I feel and act differently.

These premises help you realize your underlying thoughts and bring them to your awareness. Once you become aware, you harness the power to change them.

Let's take a closer look at John's automatic thoughts using the three-column technique from Cognitive Behavioral Therapy (CBT) to see if we can modify some of the interpretations.

A	B	C
Event	**Meaning/ Interpretatio n**	**Reaction**
Someone crossed John	Automatic Negative Thoughts	Anger—He followed, blocked the car, and screamed at the other driver. He then punched the car.
	Change the thoughts	Reaction changes

In these three columns, Column A is the event (what happened), Column B is the meaning his mind gave to the event (interpretation), and Column C is how he reacted in the form of his words, expression, and behaviors (following the other car).

You may think A (the event) caused C (the reaction). But, like in our example, A (the event) leads to B (interpretation), which led to C (reaction).

The interpretation—the meaning your mind gives to the event—acts as a mental filter and leads to a different reaction.

In the example of John, what could be the automatic thoughts that he was not aware of?

Perhaps his thoughts were:
This driver is the most disrespectful, discourteous, and uncaring person in the whole world.
Everyone cuts me off.
They think I am a loser.
No one should cut me off.
This is awful.
It is the worst possible thing that could happen to me.
This person thinks he is the only important person on the road.

He thinks that other people's time is not important.

Let's look at some of John's presumed automatic thoughts individually. You may call the negative thought an
ANT: Automatic Negative Thought, and the alternative an
APT: Automatic Positive Thought.

His first thought was: *This driver is the most disrespectful, discourteous, and uncaring person in the whole world.*
If we look closely and check the validity, John did not know the other driver at all.

The only thing he knew was that the other driver was going fast and cut him off in traffic. This driver could have been the most respectful, courteous, and caring person.

He may be so stressed and stuck in his own thoughts that he may not have realized that he was the one who was going fast and cut off another driver.

Interpreting it this way, how could John's reaction change?

A	B	C
Event	Interpretation	Reaction
	ANT: This driver is the most disrespectful, discourteous, and uncaring person in the whole world.	Anger
	APT: He may be so stressed and stuck in his own thoughts that he may not have realized that he was the one who was going fast and cut off another driver.	Let it go

His next thought was: *Everyone cuts me off. They think I am a loser.* He can ask himself, "Is that even true? Where is the proof?" On that day alone, there were many other drivers on the road who did not, in fact, cut him off.

This is called *generalization* in CBT. If he catches his thought and changes it to: *Out of 100 drivers on the road today, 99 did not cut me off. Only one did. It is not a big deal. It's not the end of the world,* he will likely stop feeling angry and will be able to move on.

A	B	C
Event	Interpretation	Reaction
	ANT: Everyone cuts me off. They think I am a loser.	Anger
	APT: Out of 100 drivers on the road today, 99 did not cut me off. Only one did. It is not a big deal. It's not the end of the world.	Less anger

John's next thought was: *No one should ever cut me off.* The word "should" is one of the most common energy-draining (maladaptive) thoughts in CBT.

Usually, when you feel upset or guilty, you may find that you are demanding something from others or yourself. Either you are expecting others to think like you or act like you, or you expect them to act according to the image you have in your mind.

Your automatic thought is: *I am right, others are wrong.* You may believe the myth that the only way to not be upset by other people is to get them to change to your way of being.

You may use words like "should" or one of its five partner demanding words like "have to," "ought to," "got to," "need to," or "must." These words imply that it is an imperative requirement that others do what you demand.

There is no choice.

When you use words like those, you are likely to feel bad, no matter what happens. You set yourself up to not be content.

For example, you tell yourself, "I should exercise." If you do exercise, you don't feel happy because you feel that it is not a big deal.

You should have done it anyway. If you don't exercise, you feel guilty because you should have done it.
So, you're not happy either way. If John says that other drivers should not cut him off, he doesn't feel particularly happy that 99 drivers who passed him earlier that day did not cut him off. But when one did, he felt the anger.

What if you changed your *"should"* to *"I would like to?"* Would you feel less angry or guilty or pressured?

Regarding exercise, if you say, *"I would like to exercise,"* and you do, you feel good because you did what you like to do. If you don't, you don't feel guilty.

A	B	C
Event	Interpretation	Reaction
	No one *should* ever cut me off	Anger
	I **would like** it if people didn't cross me	It's not a big deal

John's next thought was: *This is awful. It is the worst possible thing that could happen to me.* If you look closely, he is making the issue bigger than it is. He is using another energy-draining/maladaptive pattern called catastrophizing—or magnifying—in CBT.

He sees the event as a catastrophe when it technically is not. He is magnifying it to be much bigger than it is. If he questions himself and sees the event for what it actually is, his reaction would be less intense.

A	B	C
Event	Interpretation	Reaction
	This is awful. It is the worst possible thing that could happen to me.	Anger
	It is not awful. It is not the worst possible thing that could happen to me.	Let it go.

Another thought that was causing maladaptation for him was: *This person thinks he is the only important person on the road. He thinks that other people's time is not important.*

Here John is making assumptions about things he doesn't know and reaching a conclusion with no evidence other than the fact that this particular person cuts him off.

He doesn't know how this person treats others.

He doesn't have any idea.

John is using a pattern called black-and-white thinking or all-or-none thinking. He is assuming that a person is either caring or not caring. But in life, not everything is completely this way or that way.

There is a lot of gray area between black and white. (You can refer to the list of maladaptive cognitions in the book *Feeling Good* by Dr. David Burns).

A	B	C
Event	Interpretation	Reaction
	ANT: This person thinks he is the only important person on the road. He thinks that other people's time is not important.	Anger
	APT: I don't know if this person thinks he is the most important. I don't want to waste my time thinking about what he thinks or doesn't think. He seems to be in a hurry. It doesn't matter to me. Let me enjoy my commute.	Let it go

Sometimes, the automatic thoughts feel so true that it may seem hard to find an alternative. In that situation, you can ask yourself how energizing or draining the thought is.

Is there a less draining or more energizing thought I could have?

In John's example, he can replace the thought with: *He seems to be in a hurry. It doesn't matter to me. Let me enjoy my commute.*

Going through the previous examples, does it make sense to you that the usual assumption that whatever happens from the outside (the event: column A) doesn't directly cause your reaction: column C).

In reality, whatever happens from the outside (the event: Column A) leads to certain automatic thoughts (interpretation: column B), which leads to your reaction (column C). The interpretation—the meaning your mind gives to the event—acts as a mental filter. When you change this mental filter, it leads to a different reaction.

Choose an example from your life and use this technique. Make three columns on a page or use the worksheet available to you at http://stresstojoy.com/resources

In column A, write down the event that triggered your reaction. In Column C, write down your reaction. Your reaction could be your feeling, your words, or your behavior—or all three.

Now, for column B, ask yourself, "What were my automatic thoughts that made me feel or behave this way?" List everything that surfaces.

Once you come up with your thoughts, review each one to determine whether you have proof that the thought is true or if you are reacting to past attitudes and beliefs.

What is that belief, and is it helping you feel better (adaptive)? Or is it leading to undesirable feelings and behaviors (maladaptive)?

If it is maladaptive, what could be an alternative thought or belief that is more rational and helpful (adaptive)? You then replace your thoughts.

This thought training is your mind reprogramming. Repeating this exercise will help you reprogram your mind since you will find that your automatic thoughts will gradually become more adaptive.

When you start reflecting on your automatic thoughts in this manner, it may initially take a few days before you can process and reprogram your thoughts.

As you practice, the time between the triggering event and your ability to reflect will decrease.

You will be able to do it after a few hours, then a few minutes, and pretty soon you will be able to catch your maladaptive thoughts as they are happening, changing them to adaptive thoughts and responding differently in the moment.

From now on, be aware of your reaction. Whenever you see yourself reacting undesirably, ask yourself, "Why am I reacting in a way that is not helping me and adding to my stress?"

Identify the underlying thoughts and beliefs that are giving negative meaning to your experience and alter them to become more adaptive thoughts.

You can use the three columns to help you do that.

You can also learn more about these techniques from many books and materials available online since this is a very well-researched and popular technique.

One of the books that has helped many of my patients is *Feeling Good* by David Burns. If you would like to further understand, this is a great resource.

Now that you have learned to reprogram your mind by identifying your underlying maladaptive thoughts and replacing them with alternative adaptive thoughts, you are ready to healthily respond to your situation.

Let's explore the third R of our formula 3R with CPR in the next chapter.

Chapter 6

Respond:

How to select the best solution using your wise mind.

What is the next step after realizing your underlying thoughts and exploring the alternative ways of thinking and reacting? It is time to respond to your situation with intention.

The third R of the formula is about this **response**. This could be the way you are thinking or expressing yourself or your physical actions. When you react to a stressful situation without awareness, it is an unhealthy reaction.

That reaction, when infused with the power of awareness and intention, can become a healthy response. How do you change your unhealthy reaction to a healthy response?

Let's review that in this chapter.

Sam
Once Sam realized why she was reacting and identified her underlying thoughts and beliefs, it was time for her to respond.

She wanted to choose the alternative that made the most sense to her. Her emotional mind was pushing for the title and promotion to the position of CFO.

Her rational mind was assessing the facts (the opportunity cost in terms of money, health, and happiness). Both were pointing in two different directions.

Finally, her wise mind (the overlap between the rational and emotional mind) helped her decide.

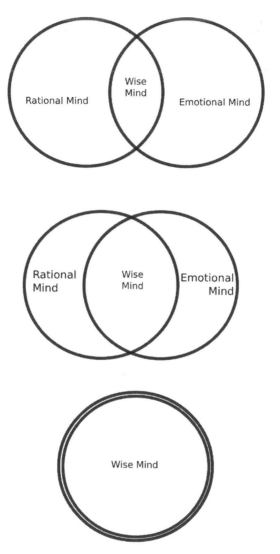

Her wise mind acknowledged her emotional desires, looked at the rational reasons, and came to the conclusion that she needs to bring balance back into her life.

If she keeps her purpose and priorities in view, she can achieve them even in her current position.

She chose to do her best during her work hours without an excessive focus on promotion, leave work at a reasonable time, enjoy her drive mindfully, exercise three times a week before work (starting her workday later on those days), and spend time with her family every evening.

In essence, after she acknowledged and calmed down, she was able to reflect. She reflected in her daily journal; she recognized the part of the stress that was coming from the outside and the part that she was contributing to by her reactions.

She realized the reason (conscious or unconscious thinking) for reacting that way and explored alternatives. She then decided how she wanted to respond with her wise mind.

She also noticed that the more she used her wise mind, the more her rational and emotional minds integrated and it became easier to make wise decisions.

Rene

Rene also explored her alternatives. She had the option to choose to stop, start, or continue her behavior. She decided to respond by developing new tools. I shared two techniques I use to offload and prioritize when I feel overwhelmed, called Brain Dump Bubbles and 5 Ds. She was able to relate and started using them.

The following week, Rene specifically came to tell me how much the technique helped her. She said that it allowed her to clear her mind and she was able to get her work done more quickly. Even her husband noticed the difference. If you would like to do these exercises that helped her, follow along.

Brain Dump Bubbles

When you find that you can't calm down due to the clutter of things that need to be done, you can also try this exercise.

When there are too many files stored on your computer, what do you do? You download them to an external drive to clear some space for processing, right?

Similarly, you can download the to-dos that are cluttering your mind space by doing this exercise. It combines the commonly used techniques of "brainstorming" and the "Brain dump technique."

I learned the brain dump technique from David Allen's book *Getting Things Done,* in which he advises recording every single to-do that may be cluttering your brain on a separate sheet of paper and then deciding on each item in the second stage of processing.

I'd done that process a few times, and it helped me a lot, but I struggled with one issue. There were so many single pieces of paper that it was overwhelming, especially because I couldn't see the whole picture at one glance.

So, I modified this exercise and I dumped all my to-dos using a brainstorming style. If you want to do that, write all your to-dos in bubbles as they come to the mind.

You make big bubbles for major projects and small bubbles for small tasks, and then connect them to the big bubbles.

Keep making these connected bubbles for each related task as it pops into your mind.

Think of all the areas of your focus. Look in all the places you keep your reminders or to-dos (phones, diaries, sticky notes, etc.).

Keep jotting down until you feel that you have downloaded all the to-dos in your mind.

When I did this exercise for the first time, I started with three big bubbles: personal, business, and professional. I started making smaller bubbles out of each area to incorporate all the to-dos that were on my mind.

After that, I also added all the other sticky notes and phone reminders that I had scattered all over. When I finished the exercise, I felt relief. The clutter was out of my head and on the paper.

It felt like a big burden was lifted from my shoulders.

The first few times, I couldn't fit everything on one page and had to spread it over three pages, but I kept them side-by-side to see the whole picture in one glance.

Now I am usually able to fit everything on one page.

Looking at it, I realized that I was trying to do too many things. No wonder I was so overwhelmed. If I did everything on that list, it would take me a whole year to finish, and here I was trying to do them in one day.

Can this exercise be overwhelming in itself?

Yes, it was...until I reflected on the fact that this was all now on paper instead of in my head. Before dumping like this, I felt that there was no end to my to-dos. After dumping, I realized that no matter how many tasks are on the list, it is still a finite number.

Once I realized that I could not possibly do all those tasks in one day, I had a choice to prioritize. A systematic approach I had learned and modified called 5 Ds helped me to prioritize.

5 Ds for Prioritizing

I used to do things in order of how they popped up in my brain or on my to-do list like most list makers do. Do you do the same? If so, you may find that you waste most of your time and energy on less important tasks leaving some important tasks incomplete. Those incomplete important tasks add to your stress.

The 5 D system can help you focus on the first things first and balance different aspects of your life: yourself vs. others, mind vs. body, or personal vs. professional. It will help you decrease demands, avoid distractions, and complete the important tasks.

To apply this technique, after you do a brain dump exercise (jotting down all the demands in your life), identify the purpose of each task by asking *why* you want to do that.

Once you identify the purpose, you can assign each task to one of these categories, based on their importance.

The Five Ds:
1. Delete
2. Diminish
3. Delegate
4. Delay
5. Do it/Deal with it

1. Delete: Some tasks may be popping up in your mind, but they are neither urgent nor important. You may like to do them, but they don't fulfill any of your life goals at this stage. Simply permit yourself to delete them.

How do you determine what is not urgent or important? Stephen Covey's **"Quadrant Thinking"** model from his book *The Seven Habits of Highly Effective People* helps me decide. Although the book focuses on management skills for leaders, you can easily apply them to managing everyday life issues. Covey says that you can divide every task into four quadrants.

1. Upper left quadrant: Urgent and important
2. Upper right quadrant: Non-urgent but important
3. Lower left quadrant: Urgent but not important
4. Lower right quadrant: Non-urgent and not important

Q1: Urgent/Important	Q2: Non-urgent/Important
Q3: Urgent/Not important	Q4: Non-Urgent/Not important

As you review how you spend your time, you may notice that a lot of your hours may be going into doing things that are urgent. They may or may not be important, but they demand your attention (email, a Facebook comment, or the first thing on your to-do list).

What happens if you address these things as they pop up?
You may end up doing things that are not that important, and there may not be any time left for important, non-urgent tasks.

You may be putting out fires all the time instead of focusing on preventing them. When the important/non-urgent tasks are left unaddressed, they soon become urgent.

Let me use a simple example from daily life to clarify.

I am specifically choosing a few tasks outside of work. Don't disregard this if you find it too simple. Follow the principle.

Let's say you have several competing activities on your day off. You want to:
· Do laundry
· Get groceries
· Make dental appointments for yourself and the kids
· Finish watching your soap opera
· Pay some bills

Ask yourself about each activity and its importance or urgency, and assign the quadrant. You would assign these to any quadrant based on your definition of what is important to you. What is important to me may not be important to you.

After using the system for some time, I can intuitively see and decide the correct quadrant in my mind, and you will also be able to do that after some practice. In our simple example:

If you have not done laundry for the whole week, laundry may fall in quadrant one; if you did it yesterday, it might be in quadrant two.

·   If you are out of food, grocery shopping may be in quadrant one. Otherwise, it's landing in quadrant two.

·   If you are making dental appointments as a preventive cleaning, it goes in quadrant two, but if your teeth are in bad shape, then it becomes a quadrant one activity.

·   If your soap opera is your addiction, and you are just watching it without thinking and feeling guilty or bad, it is quadrant four. If you have made an intentional choice and have set aside time for it to meet your goal of relaxation, then it is quadrant two.

·   If your bills are overdue, they should be in quadrant one, but if you are up to date and you need to set up payments for next month, then it is quadrant two.

Based on this thinking, you can potentially delete watching your soap opera or delay it until its designated time, so you feel good when you spend time watching it.

2. **Diminish:** Some of the demands you are not able to delete, you may be able to diminish.

I had a realization one day when I was helping my daughter with a school project. I noticed that she was more focused on decorating it than any other aspect.

Like most parents, I advised her to do the first things first (i.e., do the basic requirement/most important aspects of the project first so she can submit it on time, and spend time decorating once she finishes the important content).

I realized that even I get distracted in secondary aspects before the primary tasks and feel overwhelmed. I need to heed my own advice and diminish what is secondary.

You can also apply the same advice to your life. If you can diminish the secondary and tertiary tasks, then diminish them. Do the most beneficial parts first.

One rule that helps me decide what is primary, secondary, or tertiary is the 80/20 rule.

What is the "**80/20 rule?**"

This rule is also called the Pareto principle. It is the law of the vital few, which states that, for many events, roughly 80 percent of the effects come from 20 percent of the causes.

Although Pareto developed this concept in the context of the distribution of income and wealth among the population, it applies to many other aspects of life.

You can use the principle that 80 percent of outcomes you want come from 20 percent of your activities.

Often, I forget that principle and get back into my old habit of just writing a to-do list and doing whatever pops up in front of me.

When I start getting overwhelmed, I have to remind myself, *what are 20% of my tasks that give me 80% of the results I want?* It helps me to determine if an activity would help me achieve what is important to me. What would matter most in the long run?

You can also diminish some of the demands on your to-do list this way.

3. **Delegate:** If you cannot delete or diminish some tasks, you may try to delegate. You cannot delegate all tasks, but you can delegate many tasks to either technology or other people.

When you delegate, you may run into some issues. One issue that I struggled with was when I tried to ask someone to do a certain task, and they didn't do the work exactly as I needed. It then took more of my time to fix the problem.

Therefore, I avoided delegating for quite some time.

I always believed in the team approach. I just didn't know how to properly delegate.

Once I learned the importance of clarifying the purpose, guiding through the process and monitoring, I became a better delegator.

Another issue that I ran into was feeling guilty when I asked for help. Many people face that. My colleague Laila felt guilty asking her daughter to help with house chores when she was feeling sick.

She was feeling overwhelmed since her house was getting dirty and her laundry was piling up, yet she felt too guilty to ask for help from her teenage daughter who was working part-time and studying part-time.

She had her "aha moment" when she realized that asking her daughter to help with the chores was not just asking for a favor for herself but also doing a favor to her daughter.

Because her daughter is on the cusp of moving out to be on her own, training her daughter to take care of needed chores would be setting her up for success when she is living independently.

Yes, she is likely to learn on her own when required, but doing chores while living with her parents will help her develop the skill. It will make it much easier in the future because it will come to her automatically.

Laila needed to train her daughter on one task at a time and provide enough supervision and encouragement for her to master the task, but once she developed the habit of balancing home chores and external tasks, it helped them both in the long run.

When I asked my staff, family, or friends for something that I thought was a favor to me, I used to feel guilty.

Once I clarified the purpose of asking and gave proper instruction, support, and oversight, I felt good about letting them grow into their roles and I was less stressed myself.

Now I allow people to take care of me from time to time, since I take care of others, without feeling the guilt.

You may be able to do that as well.

4. Delay: There will be items that you can't delete, diminish, or delegate but may be able to delay. Like the example of the soap opera, if something is a quadrant 2 activity that fulfills one of your goals (like relaxation), you may schedule an appropriate time slot and delay it until then.

Often, you will find yourself in situations where you are not able to do things that you want to do. If it is possible to delay, then delay.

Sometimes, you have to delay major projects, like I had to with this book project. I wanted to get this book published a few years ago. I had to use this technique to handle various demands that came my way.
I delayed this project and picked it back up a few years later when the time was right.

So, if you find that there is a project for which there is a timeline, and you are the person who set the timeline, then you are also the person who can change it.

If possible, delay some projects/tasks for the appropriate time and place a reminder on the calendar so you don't forget.

5. **Do it/Deal with it.** After applying the previous four Ds, there will be demands left that you can choose to do. In our previous example, the groceries and the dental appointment would be two of those demands.

In summary, go through the list of your to-dos and use the 5 Ds to decide what you want to do that day, that week, or later, and put it on your calendar with a reminder system. Check to see if you can delete something. If you can't delete it, diminish it; if you can't diminish it, delegate it; if you can't delegate it, delay it; if you can't delay it, do it.

I have seen Rene and many of the people who have used this technique feel less overwhelmed.

If you don't clear your mind or prioritize, you will continue to feel overwhelmed by the unending demands.

But if you do this exercise from time to time, you will be able to focus on the most important items and feel less overwhelmed.

Go ahead and take out a few plain pieces of paper or use a template downloadable at http://stresstojoy.com/resources and dump all the tasks and projects that are on your mind using Brain Dump Bubbles.

Once down, use 5 D criteria to prioritize.

1. Delete what is not important and not urgent.

2. Diminish whatever is not part of the 20% that gives you 80% of the results.

3. Delegate what you can train someone to do or use technology to accomplish.

4. Delay what is not needed right away, but remember to put it on the future schedule so it can be done and not forgotten.

5. Do what is left. Deal with what you need to do.

These techniques will help you choose the most important tasks, decrease some of the demands, and help you focus on your chosen activities with a clear mind.

Natasha
After realizing that she didn't want to suffer twice from possible negative consequences in the future by applying the crossroad technique, Natasha responded to her worrying thoughts by developing a mantra to shift her thinking.

You can also use the mantra once you realize that the thoughts coming into your mind are not in your control, but what you do with the thoughts is in your control.

You can change the negative thought to a positive one by using these three mantras:

1. I **choose** not to suffer before suffering.

2. I **am going to** deal with the problem **if** it happens **when** it happens (since there is a chance that the negative consequence I am worried about may not happen or may only happen after a long time).

3. I **intend to focus** and do my best to get the results I want and not the results I don't want.

You can download this mantra sheet from http://stresstojoy.com/resources and post it in a prominent area to remind yourself when you start worrying.

You may notice that you feel better when you use these mantras and 5 minutes later, the negative thoughts could resurface. Again, use the mantra and shift your thinking. Gradually, 5 minutes will become 10, then 30, and then an hour.
Even though the thoughts may come back, those few minutes or hours between negative thoughts will give your brain relief.

Gradually, the time gap between the negative thoughts will increase, and the frequency of negative thoughts will decrease.

After a few days, Natasha told me she was not worrying as much since she started training her brain in this manner.

She said what helped her the most was learning that she **suffers twice** when she worries, and she didn't want that. That helps her to get motivated to stop worrying.

Due to the worrying and constant thinking pattern, Natasha also had difficulty with sleep.

She tried the basic five for falling asleep (sleep hygiene routines, relaxation exercises, light stretching, reading boring self-help books, and writing or art) which helped her most nights, but there were nights when her mind was too active to sleep despite the exercises.

What helped her on those nights was the floating Bubble meditation.

Floating Bubble Exercise
When your sleep is disturbed by too many jumpy thoughts and to-dos, this exercise can come in handy.

I had to come up with this exercise for myself one day when my mind was very active. In the past, when I had trouble sleeping, I used to write in my journal or jot down things to do on a piece of paper.

Since I started using my cell phone as a tool for reminders (in addition to many other things), I started adding thoughts to my to-do list as they popped up in my mind, even in the middle of the night.

Although it helped me to get those things done later, I faced one problem.

The phone distracted me. It invariably pulled my attention to other things, like emails and messages, due to the alerts. When my eyes caught them, I felt the urge to check.

I would briefly think about checking them, but the thought to check never vanished. One thing led to another, and my mind went off on a flurry of tangents.

I also used to write down the issues that were bothersome. Sometimes it helped me to come up with options, and other times writing the details of the bothersome event in the middle of the night was making me more awake.

I had noticed that when I jotted down even one word representing the things I wanted to do or an issue I wanted to work on, I could trick my mind into thinking that since I had noted it, I wouldn't forget, so it stopped bothering me.

I was able to sleep better most days...but not others.

I knew that writing helped me, so I needed to come up with something that could allow me to let go of my thoughts without making me feel more awake and worked up. I had learned a meditation technique called floating bubble meditation from one of my patients. Combining the two techniques, I came up with this floating bubble exercise.

I turned on a reading light and kept my diary open to a page where I drew a wave, and on top of the wave were floating bubbles.

I focused on my breath and imagined sitting with a river flowing in front of me. The bubbles on top of the wave were also passing in front of me. I was just watching them go. I didn't need to catch them; I just observed them floating pass me.

Stress to Joy

As I did the meditation, thoughts kept coming up. Every time a thought surfaced, I wrote a word to represent the thought in one of the bubbles, and then observed it as it passed.

I did not try to catch it or hold onto it. I allowed it to flow with the flow of the river. I tried to bring the focus back to my breath and the image of the floating bubble on the river.

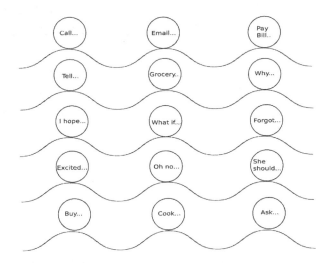

Another to-do item came to my mind, and I
wrote a word to represent that in the next
bubble to the right and allowed it to float away
to the left.

When a thought about a person came to mind
or an issue came to mind, I wrote a name or a
word to represent them and allowed them to
float past.

The thoughts kept coming, and I kept writing
in the bubbles on the next page and the next.

The morning after the first time I did this
exercise, I found that I had made forty-nine
bubbles, and the last few bubbles were illegible
because I'd fallen asleep.

The next time you find your mind too jumpy to
rest at night, open your diary or journal—or
any piece of paper—and make the thought
bubbles. You can also use the floating bubble
template that I have added to the resources at
http://stresstojoy.com/resources.

You can keep a few printed copies near your
bed to use on those nights.

Jot down one word for any thought that comes to your mind and then let it go.

See how long your mind takes to empty itself of the thoughts and becomes free of the urge to rewind over and over again.

You may also find yourself peacefully falling back to sleep most of the time.

If the idea of using a diary and reading light doesn't work for you, you may try a variant meditation of popping bubbles.

My daughter came up with that variant when I taught this technique to her one day.
She told me that what helped her was to put her thoughts in bubbles that form underwater.

She saw them rise to the top of the water and then pop. With the bubble popping, the thought was gone, and she did not realize when she fell asleep.

You may try doing that, and it may help you find some peaceful sleep.

As you practice these techniques for restful sleep, one issue may come up. You may feel upset when sleep is interrupted and you wake up in the middle of the night.

Your automatic thought may be, *I am so upset that I can't sleep. Now I will be tired in the morning. I will be late."*

By using an internal dialogue like this, you get your mind more worked up and decrease the chance of falling back into a restful sleep.

Sleep is not in your control. But what you do when insomnia strikes *is* in your control.

So, you can change the thought to, *I am up, and that is okay. I cannot force myself to sleep, but I can try my best to give my mind rest. I will fall asleep or not. Either way, it is okay. I will make the best of my time.*

By changing the internal dialogue and the meaning you give to the external event, you take away the pressure to fall asleep, thus increasing the chance of falling asleep.

Even if you don't fall asleep and still use some of the listed techniques, your mind may get partial rest—which is far better than no rest

Did you notice the third **R** of the formula that our friends used? It was to **Respond.**

The response is the way you face your life situation by using your wise mind. Sometimes this response may be different from your previous reaction and sometimes it's the same.

Even the same unhealthy reaction will become a healthy response when done with **awareness and intention.**

How are you going to respond to your stress situation?

Our three friends found that when they became aware of conflicts between their rational and emotional minds, and used their wise mind to intentionally respond to their situation, they did well.
Now they wanted to establish a new pattern of responding to future situations, so their past habits didn't creep back. They tried the second part of the formula: **CPR.**

Let's see how you can also learn this part of the formula in next chapter.

Chapter 7
Choose:

How to make new habits by declaring your choices.

Has it ever happened that you respond to one stressful situation wisely with awareness and intention, but when another life challenge arises, you react unhealthily? Do your old patterns return? That is not a surprise. It happens to many. Why?

Think about it. How old are you? That is the number of years you have had to implement your patterns of reaction. Now you are trying to establish new patterns.

You need time and practice. Some tools can help you effectively establish your new patterns. The second part, CPR, of the stress to joy formula 3R with CPR, can help you. In this chapter, let's explore the first component, **C** of CPR.

Sam
Once Sam healthily responded to her commute stress, she realized that she was still struggling with her health and relationship. Initially, she believed that she didn't have a choice in everything.

As she continued to acknowledge with mindfulness and regularly reflected in her journal, she realized that she had a choice in everything.

When she did not make a choice intentionally, the circumstances were chosen for her. She had a choice to stop or continue what she was doing.

She realized that she needed to **make and declare her choices** continuously regarding where she wanted to focus. She started writing, "I choose" statements in her journal.

Sometimes she had difficulty choosing between seemingly important options. The Rule of 10/10/10 helped her make those choices.

The Rule of 10/10/10
You can also use this rule when you can't decide between options, especially when all of them are important and make you feel overwhelmed, afraid, angry, or worried.

You ask yourself, "Would this matter in ten days?

In ten months?

In ten years?"

I first learned this rule from one of my patients, who had read it in Suzy Welch's book *10-10-10.* Although the author used it in the broader context of making life decisions, you can easily apply it in deciding your focus, thoughts, or behaviors.

I have found this to be a great question that puts things in perspective for many people. It helped Sam choose her priorities daily.

Rene

As Rene responded to the overwhelming demands of her life by brain-dumping and prioritizing with 5D, she felt better for some time.

After a while, things started piling up again. When she missed something from her many to-dos, and a client made a rude or demeaning comment, she felt emotional and had a binge eating episode.

She was getting stuck in the cycle again. She again acknowledged, calmed down, and reflected in her journal.

She realized that making those choices was not a one-time deal. She needed to continue making the healthy choices and letting go of things that bothered her.

She needed to learn a way to let go of the demeaning words that her mind kept repeating.

When someone said those words, it hurt her one time. But when she kept repeating the experience in her mind, she kept hurting herself again and again.

What someone else does is not in her control but what she does is in her control. She declared, "I choose not to hurt myself."

When I shared the camel face technique to let go of the hold of those words, we laughed a lot. It made so much sense to her that she told me, "I am going to put a camel picture on the side of my notice board.

It will remind me of my choice to let go.

Camel Face Technique :
You can also use this technique when you want
to let go of past hurtful words. You can
decrease the hurt by stopping your mind from
repeating.

Please use caution. If you have developed post-
traumatic stress disorder from the verbal
abuse, this technique may not be appropriate,
so skip it or have your therapist help you. It
works very well with the occasional harsh or
hurtful comments made by someone.

I learned this technique many years ago from a
reading course by Ed Strachar. I have modified
it and used it to help many of my patients.

One patient who came in crying left laughing.
She said it was the funniest technique. It will
make more sense if you follow along.

I will use Rene's example when someone called
her "stupid." For this exercise, replace it with
an accusatory or degrading statement from
your past that made you feel insulted or hurt.

Recall the image of that person who insulted you. In your imagination, place a funny animal face, like a camel with a drooling face, on the body of that person.

See, in your mind's eye, those demeaning words coming from the camel's mouth while drooling at the same time.

You can use your creativity and make the image even funnier, by putting funny sunglasses or a polka dot dress on the camel.

Can you take these statements seriously? Now imagine the camel saying it very fast as if you are fast-forwarding a video. Now imagine the camel saying it very slowly in a funny voice while walking backward. Now make the camel run backward while saying those words. See the camel becoming smaller and smaller until it disappears.

Do those statements hold the same power over you as before?

Most of the time, you will find that either the statements will stop bothering you or make you laugh. Either way, they won't have the same powerful hold on you as before.

The next time anyone starts saying demeaning things to you, you can do this technique right at the moment.

Bring the image of the camel to your mind and imagine it on top of the body of the person who is saying demeaning words.

You will notice that you won't feel as offended. The other person may feel offended if you start laughing at their comments though, so use discretion.

But there is no reason to take those words seriously. It is their garbage. If someone puts garbage in your space, do you keep it and suffer from the smell or throw it away?

Why would you allow the garbage coming from someone's mouth into your heart?

Natasha
After Natasha used her wise mind to healthily respond to her frustrations, she felt good. She wanted to continue to feel good and didn't want her worry and anger habit to come back.

She realized that these feelings are like families. You invite one negative feeling, and pretty soon the whole family of negative feelings starts visiting you more.

She declared, "**I choose to** behave like water and not milk in the heat of stress." **When milk boils, it spills** over and messes up the stove. (I hate to clean the stove afterward, and it is so hard to remove the stains from frequent spills).

When water boils, it rises above.
It changes into steam. It changes form. It becomes pure. **Even when it spills, it extinguishes the fire.**

Before she learned to manage her stress, Natasha used to think that expressing anger was the best way to deal with it.

Her experiences had taught her differently.

She agreed with the research that expressing anger in certain ways can lead to more harm than good.

After losing her temper and saying or doing things in anger, she usually felt embarrassed, ashamed, and angrier. She rarely got what she wanted by blowing up, or if she got it, she felt too angry to enjoy it.

The other person involved (many times someone she cared about) walked away mad. The situation got worse when the other person held a grudge and waited for revenge or took it out on others.

So, Natasha declared her choice. When she felt the anger building, she calmed down with a deep, **cooling breath**.

With this kind of breathing, you breathe in through your mouth while curling up your tongue as if you are sipping from a straw, and feel the coolness in your mouth.

She excused herself from the scene for a few seconds and walked to a place where she could get some water (refrigerator or fountain or water bottle).

She sat down and drank the water. She counted to seven or said a prayer in her heart. She found that this process allowed her to calm her mind and give her a few precious moments to choose a wise response.

Both acts of sitting and drinking water can calm the mind. When she was angry, her mind could not think properly, and she had a knee-jerk reaction.

She said and did things that she later regretted. When she was calm, she was able to think and had the opportunity to choose her response wisely.

During these times, **Seeing the Big Picture** helped. Once I was visiting her and she was feeling very upset with a colleague's email. She was getting angrier each day.

She was so worked up about the issue that she was fuming over it for several days and nights. It was disturbing her sleep.

We had the following dialogue, which helped her. Imagine you are Natasha here and I am your friend. Insert the issue that you are feeling frustrated about in place of Natasha's issue and go through the following dialogue.

185

Natasha: I am feeling disgusted.

Rozina: Why? What happened?

Natasha: I am so frustrated with this…I keep thinking about it. It's keeping me up at night.

Rozina: How big is this problem in the grand scheme of your life?

At the time, she was feeling so angry, she answered, "It is very big."

Rozina: Really? Out of all the things that affect your life, how big of an effect does this event have? Estimate it as a percentage.

Natasha: Maybe 30 percent.

So, we looked closer and used this logical deduction:

Rozina: What is your life expectancy?

Natasha: Eighty to one hundred years.

Rozina: How long would this issue matter? Ten days? Ten months? Ten years?

Natasha: 10 days, probably.

Rozina: Let's say that you are going to live for one hundred years. Then the current year is 1 percent of your life. Right?

If this issue would matter for 10 days and there are 365 days in a year, that is 0.027%. That means this issue is going to matter less than 0.03% of this year, which is 1 percent of your life.

Natasha: Right.

Rozina: Are there other important things in your life this year? What are they?

Natasha: Yes...my health, my family, my home, my car, my job, my beautiful surroundings.

Rozina: These are all important things in your life. Compared to all these important things that matter in your life, how important is this incident in the grand scheme of life?

Natasha: Point zero, zero, three percent.

Rozina: Are the time, mental energy, and focus you are giving this issue in proportion to how big the issue is? When you get stirred up like that, your adrenaline level goes up.

Your blood pressure goes up, which can lead to a heart attack or stroke.

Your stomach acid goes up, which leads to the risk of an ulcer. Isn't it like punishing yourself? Why would you risk a heart attack or stroke or peptic ulcer for something or someone that you don't even like?

You get the point. Initially, Natasha thought that the event was very big.

Then she realized that it was as big as 30 percent and finally, she realized that it was no more important than 0.003% in the grand scheme of her life.

She realized that her reaction was way bigger than the event required and was occupying 90 percent of her focus that day.

Once she realized this, she chose to let go.

From these stories, did you guess what the **C** is in the stress to joy formula 3R with CPR? **Choice.**

Regardless of your circumstances, you always have a choice. There is a choice to focus on opportunities for improvement, a choice to throw away garbage coming out of other people's mouths, and a choice to let go of your worries, fears, and anger.

The choice of how to respond to any challenge is in your hands.

Declare your choice. Declaring establishes the choice in your brain.

When you don't consciously choose, you are allowing the circumstances to choose for you.

You are choosing to continue by default. When you choose to focus on something one time, it helps.

But the benefits don't last unless you regularly choose your focus, especially until it becomes second nature.

One way to establish a new pattern is to declare your choice. Every time you want to make a major shift in your approach, you declare, "I choose to..."

What is the second way you can make a new pattern of responding become second nature? Let's learn that second component, **P** of **CPR**, in the next chapter.

Chapter 8
Practice:

How to master the new skills by establishing new brain pathways.

Have you noticed that when you are trying to change something or learn a new skill, it feels hard? Once you master a skill, it becomes easier. But how do you master a skill?

When you establish new brain pathways, the new skills become second nature. The component, P, of the stress to joy formula 3R with CPR, can help you establish those brain pathways.

Let's learn how, with our friends' examples.

Sam
When Sam started mindfully driving, it was initially hard. She forgot to remain mindful many days. It was hard to change the way she did things for so many years.

She was comfortable in her routines. But she had chosen to change since her old patterns were not working for her.

She wrote on the front page of her journal the declaration, "I choose to be mindful and keep the purpose in my mind in all my actions."

She looked at that page every day as she did her journaling.

To help her remember her intention the whole day, she kept other small reminders around her.

She placed a hanger on her car's rearview mirror, which reminded her to practice mindfulness every time she sat in the car.

She placed some paintings in her environment that reminded her of the purpose of her work. To change her routine, she regularly **practiced** mindfulness.

As she practiced, she was able to establish her new routine. She started noticing that it became easier for her as she practiced. She also found herself becoming more mindful of other activities.

She persisted in setting boundaries between work and personal time. Although she did not have any time for her art projects yet, she started thinking creatively about other activities of daily living, like cooking.

She started seeing cooking as a form of art.

She persisted in her choice to see all experiences as Opportunities For Improvement (OFI).

Sam looked for ways to change her work and found some projects that she could do from home. She practiced making the best out of her current situation.

Through her practice, she was relaxed when she reached work, was able to keep a smile on her face, be more creative in her problem-solving skills, and be more productive in her work.

When she was more present-minded with her family, her evenings became a source of joy and relationship building. As Sam spent more time with awareness, she felt that she was living more and fully experiencing all the beautiful aspects of life.

Rene
Once Rene chose her best option to cope with her situation, she declared in her journal, "I choose to regularly practice my organization techniques."

She intentionally made a routine of organizing and planning every week. Every Sunday evening or Monday morning, she spent an hour on her weekly planning when she reviewed her major projects and divided the tasks over the following week.

She made a morning routine to look at the priorities of the day after writing in her gratitude journal and before starting her busy day.

As she persistently practiced her routine, it became easier.

She routinely practiced walking for 15 minutes while listening to her favorite songs. The days when she felt frustrated, having this routine helped.

Her practice allowed her to let out her frustration in a constructive manner and decreased the urges for emotional eating.

As she became more mindful while eating, she was able to taste the food better, she chewed properly, got more nutrition from her food, ate less, lost weight, and her eating became a source of joy again.

Natasha
Once Natasha chose her best response, she declared, "I choose to let go of my need for control." She intentionally practiced. She liked the serenity prayer by Reinhold Niebuhr used in AA (Alcoholics Anonymous):

"God, grant me the serenity to accept the things I cannot change, the courage to change the things I can, and the wisdom to know the difference."

She wrote the serenity prayer on smaller posters and placed those posters in several places, both at work and at home, as a reminder of her choice, and she chose to let go daily.

What do you think the component **P** of CPR represents? **Practice**. Each time you practice something, you strengthen the brain pathways. It is like gradually reprogramming your brain.

Simple reminders and routines help you remember to practice until you master the skill. The more you practice, the easier it gets.

How does practice make a task easier? Take, for example, a pathway in the wilderness. When someone tries to go through the wilderness the first time, a faint pathway is made.

When more people walk on the same pathway, it gets more defined, and it becomes easier for other people to walk on it. Similarly, your brain forms new pathways.

When you do something for the first time, the neurons in your brain start making connections and form pathways. When you repeat that action, more connections are made.

The more you repeat that action, the stronger those pathways become. Your brain gradually molds to these new pathways since it is more like soft dough than concrete. It's remodeled with new ideas.

This ability to mold and change is called neuroplasticity, which allows your brain to mold and train.

In the same way, as an athlete trains his or her body, you can train your thoughts, emotions, and behaviors with **Practice**.

If your mind is questioning the power of practice to master a new skill, consider how many complex patterns you have mastered in your life: walking, talking, eating, etc. Do you know how many decisions your mind is making to do these simple tasks?

Yet, you do them so easily.

Observe a child attempting to walk, and you will realize that when you started learning to walk, you needed to focus on balancing your body, standing upright, looking around, and balancing on one foot while moving the other.

Your mind had to quickly make these decisions. Once you learned, you walked without thinking about all the steps. How did you learn that? Do you even think about it anymore? No, because now it has been programmed into your brain.

You have practiced it so many times that your brain knows the complex steps needed to help you walk.

How can you practice? By setting routines and reminders. By being persistent in your practice, you can ensure those pathways get stronger. You may use pictures or artwork that will remind you.

Writing in your journal can help you remind yourself of your intention.

With our technologically advanced times, smartphones and iPads are great tools to keep certain reminders as well.

Like the pathway in the wilderness formed by people walking, it's always there. But if people stop walking, the grass will grow and hide it. Similarly, if you don't practice a new habit, the old habits will dominate.

You have trained your mind to react in a certain pattern over many years of your life. If you want to change those patterns, you will need to *train your mind* with practice.

You will need to practice frequently and persistently, so your chosen response becomes your new pattern.
Since there is only a split second between something happening (an event) and your reaction, you are likely to repeat your habitual reaction unless you have practiced staying aware.

If you practice the new habits, it will be easier.

You will be able to think, feel, and do what you have consciously chosen in the moment.
Pr-**act**-ice means **act** repeatedly. No action, no practice, no benefit.

So, Practice, Practice, and Practice until you master the skill.

In this chapter, you learned how to train your brain so you can choose your wise response in a split second.

With practice, you will be able to automatically choose the new response with little effort because you will have established new neuronal pathways in your brain.

There is one more way to increase your chances of establishing a new, healthier habit. This is represented by the **R** in CPR of the stress to joy formula: 3R with CPR.

What is it? Let's learn in the next chapter.

Chapter 9

Reinforce:

How to strengthen your new ways with this special ingredient.

When you are cooking something important, you add a certain spice to enhance the taste. What is that extra ingredient in your stress-to-joy practice? Let's learn from our three friends.

Sam

Sam was practicing mindful driving, setting boundaries, and watching and modifying her self-dialogue. She used the little car hanger that reminded her to drive mindfully.

She had seen children getting excited about things when they got stars.

To reinforce her practice, every time she drove mindfully to work, she started giving herself a star on her calendar. She began saying, "Good job for driving mindfully. I feel good when I drive like that."

During her break time, she started making a collage of pictures representing how she was making a difference in peoples' lives when she was relaxed and felt balanced in her own life.

She reinforced her practice by telling me and sharing it with her family and coworkers. The more she reinforced, the stronger she became in her new habit.

Rene

As Rene was practicing her chosen response, she reinforced her practice by both positive and negative reinforcement. She gave herself an imaginary 'pat on the back' after she did her weekly planning.

Every time she chose to walk instead of eating emotionally, she rewarded herself in constructive ways. She called a friend to set up a lunch or downloaded a favorite song. These rewards increased her desire to practice more.

Every time she gave in to emotional eating, she took away her privilege to watch her favorite TV program. To reinforce further, she picked a picture of herself at her desired body weight and posted it on her bathroom mirror.

Every time she saw it, she visualized how good it would feel when she could be healthy like that again. It helped her but she also noticed her old tendency to feel defeated about not being there yet.

To overcome the feeling of failure, instead of focusing on what she wasn't able to achieve, she started acknowledging what she was able to achieve.

When she made a goal of 10,000 steps per day, she reinforced small achievements by acknowledging. Before choosing this approach, if she only did 7,000 steps, she used to focus on the 3,000 steps she wasn't able to take and felt like a failure.

After choosing this approach, she started focusing on her achievements first, then identified the challenges, and made a plan to overcome.

She also started asking herself why she wanted to achieve a particular goal. In the case of her goal of 10,000 steps a day, she added the purpose of the goal (i.e., optimum health).

Then she gave herself a pat on the back for achieving 70% of her goal. Only after this acknowledgment did she focus on the challenges that prevented her from achieving the remaining 30% of her goal. She wrote:

Goal: 10 thousand steps each day for optimum health and happiness
Achieved: 7 thousand steps taken—70% achieved. Yeah! Good job.
Challenge: 30% short of the goal due to less scheduled time in my busy day.

Plan: Add a 15-minute walk to the lunch break.

This technique is called: **Opportunity for Improvement. (OFI)**. It allowed her to reinforce her chosen response with positive feedback, which she got by focusing on her achievement first.

It also helped her to focus on feeling happy rather than being younger or of that particular weight. She felt motivated to continue her new way of responding to her circumstances.

Natasha
Since the crossroad technique helped Natasha so much, she placed the crossroad diagram and her mantras on her refrigerator. It reminded her to shift her focus every time her mind started worrying.

She reinforced her new behavior by giving herself the reward of sitting by a nearby lake for a few minutes. She loved looking at the ducks and water lilies.

From these stories, what did you guess what makes the **R** in CPR? **Reinforce.**
Practicing new habits becomes stronger when you **reinforce with reminders and rewards**.

In these examples, our friends were losing the desire to continue their practice after some time.
They were forgetting. Once they added reminders and rewards as reinforcements, it helped them continue their practice.

Anything that you practice develops new pathways in the brain, but they can be established more efficiently when appropriately reinforced.

I learned the importance of rewards from my daughter. I used to play Sudoku with her, and every time she completed a puzzle, I gave her a star or wrote, "Good job!" One time, I forgot to give her a star.

She said, "Mom, you haven't given me a star." I suggested, "Why don't you give yourself a star?" She started doing that after solving each puzzle and felt very proud of herself.

I wondered why I didn't appreciate myself like that. Adults tend to complain when they don't get appreciated yet they forget that they can appreciate themselves.

When you are in a leadership position—a supervisor, employer, teacher, parent, etc.— you are expected to appreciate your employees, your students, and your kids, but you rarely get recognized.

When I realized that, I started appreciating myself. The days when I finish all of my chartings on time, I write on my day sheet "Good job, Rozina!" I feel like a child, but it makes me feel good.

You can also reinforce your chosen behavior with rewards, even if you feel too old. Everyone has a child inside. Nurture your inner child by rewarding yourself for good behavior.

What will you do to reinforce your practice, going forward?

If you don't reinforce your new behavior, you may not have the desire to practice, your practice may wither, and the old habits may come back.

On the other hand, if you appropriately reinforce your behavior, you will feel more motivated to continue.

Let me reinforce your persistence of sticking with the book up to this point. "Good job!" You have made it to the stress reduction part of the stress to joy system.

Before we move on to happiness-building habits, let me share one more example to summarize how Natasha applied the system to a different situation that came up shortly after she had learned it.

Natasha was worried about her daughter's decision about where to go to college. She **acknowledged** that she was stressing about her daughter making a wrong decision to go to an out-of-state college.

She **calmed down** with belly breaths.

Then she **reflected** on her situation by talking to me and writing in her journal. She used the 3R formula. She **recognized** what was inside her circle of influence and what was not.

Which college her daughter chose was of concern to her but not in her control. She could influence the decision by talking to her daughter, advising her, and sharing the pros and cons of each alternative, but it was not in her control to make that decision.

Her daughter's final decision was ultimately coming from outside of her circle. The way she was reacting to her daughter's decision was coming from inside of her circle.

Her reaction of anger, fear, and forcefulness was adding to her stress. She was using negative words and demanding tones. It was neither helping her nor her daughter.

When she asked herself why she was reacting that way, she **realized** her underlying fears. The fears from her past experiences were leading to her automatic thoughts. She was future-reading that her daughter was making the worst decision.

She thought only about the negative consequences of her daughter's decision, without anticipating any possible positive outcomes (black and white thinking).

She was making it bigger than it was (catastrophizing).

She looked at alternative thoughts to the maladaptive thoughts that were not helping her.

She realized that she could change her thought from *It is the worst possible decision* to *There are some benefits and some consequences of this decision* or *There could be some benefits since many kids grow emotionally and socially and learn to take responsibility when they make their own decisions.*

She could choose to think, *"My daughter is showing leadership skills by considering all input, making her decision, and standing by her decision"*, or *"She could be more successful with these skills, be able to get better jobs, and will be able to pay the loan back".*

Or maybe, *"If she is happy, she will excel in her education.*

With the change in her thoughts, my friend became open to the possibility. *"What if this is the best decision of my daughter's life?"*

Once she realized her underlying thoughts and alternatives, she decided to **respond** by focusing on what was most important to her. Her priority was her daughter's best interest and happiness.

So, she chose to focus on her daughter's happiness instead of trying to force her own decision on her daughter. She became more open to listening and appreciating her daughter.

Both of them felt happier and were able to arrive at a good decision together.

After a few days, her past attitude started creeping back. She had the worrisome thoughts again. So, she needed to take a further step to make her **choice** her new pattern. She declared her choice by writing, "I choose to focus on my daughter's happiness."

She **practiced** her response by making a flash card of her decision and putting it in her daily journal as a reminder.

She caught her thoughts when the fear came up. She acknowledged and discussed the alternative thoughts.

Her daughter was able to open up.

My friend placed a photo of her daughter's smiling face on her mirror and that helped her **reinforce** and focus on her daughter's happiness. Her daughter's excitement also helped her reinforce her new pattern.

In this way, what she learned from the stress to joy system she was able to apply in many other situations in her life that decreased her stress and increased her joy.

You can also apply what you've learned. When facing a stressful situation, you can apply the three basic steps of stress to joy:

ACR: Acknowledge, Calm Down, and Reflect. Use your tool for reflection (journal or talking to a friend), reflect on your situation, and then use the formula **3R with CPR**: Recognize, Realize, and Respond with Choice, Practice, and Reinforcement.

You can download a summary sheet of these steps for a reminder from http://stresstojoy.com/resources

So, what is your stress level now? How is the balance in your Emotional Coping Account?

If you have applied the techniques you have learned, you will notice that you don't feel as stressed.

The balance in your Emotional Coping Account may be starting to increase, but you want to have a good reserve for unexpected situations.

Therefore, you don't want to stop at just decreasing the stress. You want to further build your level of joy.

Are there habits that can help you do that?

Yes. Let's explore some of these happiness habits in next chapter to help you increase your joy and become more resilient so you can face any situation that life presents.

Chapter 10
C.O.M.P.A.S.S.
How to enhance happiness and resilience with 7 key habits.

When you master stress, you feel less "bad," but you don't want just to feel "less bad." You want to feel "really good." You want to feel joy and peace most of the time so you can be the best version of yourself. How can you do that?

A friend commented after reading my Tips for Happiness: "I thought that you feel happy when something good happens. I didn't know that happiness is a habit that you can develop."

Yes.

Happiness is a habit, and you can develop it by developing certain approaches in life. Many approaches enhance your level of joy and make you feel the happiest you could be. In this chapter, I have shared some of those profound habits.

I have grouped them using the acronym COMPASS, to help you remember the most important ones. As a compass helps you move in the right direction, these habits will show you how to move from the state of stress to the state of joy.

Let's see how our three friends are trying to develop these habits.

COMPASS-C

Sam

As Sam's stress level decreased, her skin condition started healing.

As she continued to relax and reflect, she identified that although she is very kind to other people, she is not as kind to herself.

The way she puts herself down for simple mistakes and the way she treats herself is never the way that she treats others. She cared more about others than herself and sacrificed her own interests for the benefit of others.

Caring for others was part of her value system and her purpose in life, so she didn't want to stop it. But when she got sick, she could not care for others. She identified that her tendency to not care for herself was leading to her lack of health and happiness.

Her own mind, body, and soul were her biggest assets for fulfilling her purpose. She realized that unless she fills her own bucket, she wouldn't have anything left to fill other peoples' buckets.

Unless she was healthy and happy, she could not make other people happy. She wanted to make a difference in other peoples' lives as long as she lived.

So, she reflected on her options. She decided and declared that she would treat herself with as much care as she treated others.

She hung a poster in her workplace that read, "I can help people more when I take care of myself." She forgave herself for past mistakes. She became kind to herself.

She realized that she was not laughing very much, so she started reading jokes and shared these jokes to help her laugh more.

She walked mindfully between projects and paid particular attention to eating and sleeping. She started practicing **self-compassion.**

Do you see the same pattern in your life? Taking care of others and putting other peoples' needs first is one of the values that make us human so you don't need to give that up.

You just need to achieve a balance between self-care and the care of others.

I have seen many people forget to be compassionate with themselves and neglect their self-care, which affects their ability to be compassionate with others. I was once talking to a woman sitting next to me on a flight.

She shared that she takes care of her elderly parents, her kids, and her job. For a few years, her elderly parents had been having more and more problems managing living alone and all of her time was going to helping them.

Writing used to help her feel good, but since her responsibilities had increased, she had not had the opportunity to write. She confessed that she felt guilty if she did anything to take care of herself.

She felt that she needed to take care of something all the time instead of sitting and writing to feel good.

I asked her, "Do you feel guilty when you fill the gas in your car? If you apply the same approach, should you keep driving to reach your destination in time instead of stopping to fill the gas?"

No. You stop for gas. Why? If you don't fill the gas tank regularly, you wouldn't be able to make it to your destination.

Similarly, without taking care of yourself, you can't take care of others. You need to fill your tank, your bucket, and your Emotional Coping Account so you can fill others'. Happy people practice **compassion** for the *self* in addition to compassion for *others*.

So, what is the C in the happiness acronym, COMPASS? Compassion. When you are not compassionate with yourself, you feel unhappy, and your health suffers. You become bitter and can't enjoy serving others.

When you are kind and compassionate with yourself, you can be kind and compassionate to others. So, it's important to internally develop a balance between compassion for self and compassion for others.

COMPASS-O

Natasha
Natasha realized that due to her education, experience, and position, sometimes she was not open to new ideas.

She also had an underlying belief that she should know everything.

She was getting trapped in the web of "I know." She noticed that her mind's tendency to think that it knows everything blocks her ability to learn and to enjoy the simple pleasures of life.

That kind of approach was not only causing dullness in her life but was also adding to her frustration and stress.

She decided and declared that she was going to keep her mind open and observe intentionally. She started seeing the world as if she were seeing it for the first time.

When she saw her child enjoying simple things like popping bubbles and flying birds, she decided to intentionally experience everything like a child—through the prism of a beginner's mind. She intentionally started taking every experience as an opportunity to learn.

She tried to listen more and became open to new ideas. She also became more flexible.

She learned more and improved many aspects of her life. Even when someone criticized her, she took it as an opportunity for growth. She became growth-minded. She started to intentionally develop open-mindedness.

What is the O in the happiness acronym, COMPASS? **Open-mindedness**. Happy people are open-minded. If you are not open-minded, you block any happiness coming to you.

When you are, you open the doors of joy, peace, and growth and can become the best version of yourself.

So, start observing with all your senses. Hear, smell, taste, and feel everything with open-mindedness.

COMPASS-M

Sam

When Sam watched Queen Latifah's movie, "Last Holiday," she had a realization. In the movie, the actress gets a wrong diagnosis and doctors tell her that she has six months left to live.

The actress pulls out her bucket list and starts living the life she always wanted to live.

Sam realized that each moment is important since no one knows which one could be the last. Once it's gone, it is gone forever. She realized that she doesn't need a death sentence to realize how important each day is.

No one knows when this journey will end.

People on the flights on 9/11 did not have any idea that it would be their last day. But when they realized that they were going to die, what did they do? They did what was important to them.

They called their loved ones to express their love, appreciation, make apologies, and say goodbye.
Sam decided to live and experience each moment. Her mindfulness practice helped her do that and bring more joy into her life.

She also made a habit of telling her loved ones daily, **"I love you," "Thank you," and "I'm sorry."**

What is the M in the happiness acronym, COMPASS? Mindfulness and giving importance to each **Moment of life.**
When you don't value each moment, you feel like life is passing by and you lose precious opportunities for feeling joy.

When you develop a habit of seeing each moment as new and valuable, you experience and embrace it, and your life becomes exciting and a source of joy and peace.

Each moment becomes a gift and a bonus. So, live and experience each moment with awareness and don't wait until it's too late.

At the end of each day, week, month, year, and whenever possible tell people you care about, "**I love you," "thank you," and "I'm sorry."**

COMPASS-P

Rene had started a volunteer project because she wanted to feel inner joy.

She noticed that she got so absorbed in the details of her work that she was not feeling the joy and passion with which she had taken on that project.

With her mindfulness and reflection practice, she realized that the reason for her loss of joy was due to her forgetting the purpose.

She knew that when she forgets the purpose, it robs her of the opportunity to enjoy.

So, she reminded herself of the purpose of taking that project, and it allowed her to let go of the frustration of drowning in details and start enjoying the volunteering again.

Rene started questioning the purpose in everything she undertook, including all personal projects.

She started asking herself, "Why I am doing this?" When she wrote her goals, she wrote why she wanted to achieve that goal. That purpose focused thinking helped her feel happy and flexible.

Do you ever find yourself in a similar situation? Does asking "why" help you get back on track?

Focusing on the purpose helped me a few years ago when I went on a two-week vacation with my family.
Usually, I carry some basic supplies in a carry-on, but that time we decided to fly comfortably and put all of our clothes and supplies in one big luggage bag.
We enjoyed walking without lugging a carry-on around the airport, and we enjoyed our flight. But when we reached the destination airport, the situation changed. We waited at the baggage claim for a long time.

Everyone was picking up their bags, but our luggage did not arrive. When all of the bags were taken off the belt, we talked to the support office.

We learned that the luggage was loaded on the wrong flight and we may not get it for a couple of days. We all started getting worried and upset.

As I became aware that my stress level was rising, I told myself to calm down. I took a deep breath and let go of any tension. I reflected and reminded myself of my teaching.

I asked, "What is the purpose of this vacation?"
We wanted to have fun with the family.
We were having fun.
Why are we stopping the fun if one thing goes against our plans?

I declared, "We are going to have fun, no matter what."

It took some time, but we all calmed down and went shopping. It was a late night, but we needed some basic supplies before going to the hotel.

Yes, there was frustration about wasting time and money against the plan, but what were our options?

Spoil our mood and waste the opportunity to enjoy, or do what needs to be done and achieve the purpose of vacation, which was to have fun?

We chose option two.

If this had happened before I developed the stress-to-joy system and purpose-focused thinking, I would have been so upset and bitter that I would have spoiled the whole vacation focusing on what went wrong.

When I used my wise mind and focused on purpose, I was able to enjoy the moment despite the seemingly stressful circumstance.

Therefore, when you remember the purpose, even when things don't go as planned—even if you have to take a detour—you can still reach the destination.

Many people plan a lot, but sometimes in the detailed planning, they forget the purpose.

You may spend a lot of time planning a party for your kid, but if you forget the purpose and make the kid unhappy, there is no point in planning and investing your time and resources, is there?

Purpose provides the fuel, drive, and reason to reach a destination. It provides you with the power because you are making an internal decision—an intention.

Therefore, when you add a reason to your goal, you can call it an intention statement. When your brain knows the purpose, it can adjust and find detours if needed and increase the chance you'll achieve your desired results.

A clear purpose not only makes it easier for the brain to follow what you want but also increases your level of joy in doing whatever you are doing.

The story of an old woman and three men laying bricks clarifies this point beautifully. It goes this way:

An old woman was passing by a construction site where three men were laying bricks for some kind of a wall.

She asked the first man what he was doing. He said with irritation, "Don't you see, I am laying the bricks. I do this all day, every day. Go away. Don't bother me."

She went to the second person and asked the same question. He said, "I am doing a job that pays me so I can take care of my family."

She went to the third person and asked the same question. He said, "I am so excited that I am building a beautiful church. People will come here and will find peace. I am fulfilling the purpose of my life."

Do you see the difference in perspective? Can you guess which person finds joy and which person finds stress from the same work? Can you find the purpose and passion in whatever you do?

Find the purpose. Review why you do what you do and what ways you can improve. You will find the work a source of joy, and it will give you the resilience to cope with constant deadlines, changes, or other work stressors.

What is the P in the happiness acronym, **COMPASS? Purpose-focused thinking.**

You can nurture this habit by asking 'why' for any goal, tasks, or activities you undertake. If you don't ask 'why'—the purpose—you may feel empty and unhappy even after achieving your goal.

If you don't develop a routine or habit of reflecting on the purpose, either in the form of journaling or other forms, you will find that you may forget the purpose, especially during stressful times.

If you do make a habit of keeping the purpose in mind, you will feel fulfilled even if you don't exactly get what you initially wanted and had to take a detour.

It will give you the courage to overcome fear and the motivation to stand up, even if you fall.

I suggest that you make it a routine every few months to visit the purpose of your work and revive the feeling of passion and adjust your perspective if it is wavering.

COMPASS-A

Rene
Rene used to have a very hard time accepting that things didn't go as planned, especially when she had put a lot of effort in a project. One time she asked, "The word 'acceptance' confuses me sometimes. If I accept something, does that mean that I have to give up on improving?

Does it mean that I should be happy when I lose something or someone dear to me?"

No, acceptance doesn't mean that you stop improving or should be happy and start jumping with joy when you lose a loved one. That would be unnatural.

Acceptance is the next step after awareness and acknowledgment.

To clarify the concept of acceptance, I like to modify the idiom, "Don't cry over spilled milk" by adding "Acknowledge, clean it up, and find something else to drink."

It means to **accept** the present reality, explore possible options, make a choice, and move on. *What can be more insane than not accepting what already is?*

Without accepting what *already is*, you cannot change.

You may or may not like what is happening, it may or may not be in your control, but acceptance allows you to focus your energy on what you can do about it rather than just feeling stuck.

Let me share a simple example. One day I was driving alone to a seminar in another city. I took the wrong exit and thought I could find my way, but I couldn't. My GPS was not working.

I managed to find an entrance to the freeway, but I couldn't figure out whether I should go north or south to reach my destination. I got upset and started worrying about not making it to my seminar.

I parked the car and called my husband. I was so worked up, that I started offloading on him as soon as he picked up the phone. I said, "I'm so upset that I got lost.

Now I'm not going to be able to make it to the seminar in time. All the attendees will be angry. The organizer will be upset. I am disappointed."

My husband asked, "Where are you?"
I was so worked up, I kept going on and on. I kept talking about how awful it was that I got lost.
He said, "Calm down and observe where you are. Do you want to stay stuck or get where you want to go?"

That was true. My husband could not help me until I calmed down and accepted where I was.

I looked around, gave him the information about what signs I saw, and then he could advise me on which way to go.

> *Until I accepted where I was, I was not able to move where I wanted to go.*

Remember the serenity prayer?
God, grant me the serenity to accept the things I cannot change, the courage to change the things I can, and the wisdom to know the difference.

Beautifully and succinctly, it conveys the message to become aware and accept what you cannot change and then make your best effort to change what is possible within your limitations or circumstances.

So how do you develop this attitude? Use these **"five golden principles of happiness"** that I learned from my teacher, Alwaiz Kamaluddin:

1. If you like something and it is within the circle of your moral values, enjoy it.

2. If you don't like something, and you can get rid of it, then get rid of it. (e.g., a painting in your house that you don't like).

3. If you can't get rid of it, but you can change it, then change it (e.g., the placement of furniture in your house).

4. If you can't change something (like your family), then accept it.

5. When you accept something, accept it as if it is your choice. Unless you change your attitude and get rid of the grudge, you have not fully accepted it. To not accept it will rob you of your peace and happiness.

What does **A** stand for in the happiness acronym of COMPASS? **The attitude of acceptance and gratitude**.

If you don't develop this attitude of acceptance and gratitude, you are at risk of feeling stuck and feeling the grudge. If you do develop this attitude, you will be happy, no matter what life presents to you.

Start developing this habit today by picking any situation in your life you are having difficulty accepting, and ask yourself:

· Do I like it? If the answer is Yes, then enjoy, if not, ask...
· Can I get rid of it? If yes, get rid of it, if not, ask...
· Can I change it? If yes, change it. If not, then accept it. Don't do this grudgingly, but with the attitude that it is the best thing for me. Now, what can I do to adjust and move on in life?

COMPASS-S
Natasha noticed that sometimes she was waiting for big things to happen to feel happy. She was getting happy when she went on vacation or had a big achievement, but those things happened only occasionally.

Every day felt ordinary. One time I asked, "How are you?" She said, "Same old, same old. Nothing special, nothing extraordinary."

We discussed the extraordinariness of that ordinary moment when we were talking as friends. To be able to stand, you need to have your legs and your body's balance.

To be able to talk, your ears need to be able to hear what your friend is saying, your mind needs to be able to understand language, form thoughts, and remember words to express; your mouth muscles need to be able to articulate, and your vocal cords and lungs need to produce the sound for a voice.

Thousands of neurons and body systems have to work together in your body to achieve this miracle of being able to stand and talk.

Plus, having a friend and a time and a place to talk are all additional seemingly insignificant, "nothing new, same old-same old" gifts that are playing their role in this simple act. Do you realize that?

Sometimes, you may not realize the significance of seemingly small gifts and abilities because they have been working smoothly most of your life.

You don't realize until they stop working. I didn't realize that until my dominant hand stopped working for some time.

Before that, I had never appreciated how a small bone in the wrist could affect my life so drastically. When your dominant hand goes out of commission, you are not able to do the simple activities that you take for granted like changing your clothes.

Once I realized that, it changed my life.

Once I appreciated the significance of this simple gift of my hand and the ability to write, I started writing in my gratitude journal daily. When I can't journal other things, I write a few words of gratitude without which my day feels empty.
Now I recommend writing to everyone who can because you don't have to wait until you lose your hands to appreciate the simple gift of being able to write.

Rene used to feel the need to correct her kids' mistakes, so they learn the right way. But in the process, she realized that she forgot to appreciate the significance of the most important people in her life.

She was able to relate and apply a "**3-minute No Criticism Rule**" that I had learned from Dr. Sood's book *Mayo Clinic Guide to Stress-Free Living*.

When I used to come home after a stressful day, I used to ask my kids why the bag was on the floor or shoes were in the wrong place, or why they had not done what they were supposed to do.

As I reflected, I realized that many times that was because I was stuck in my thoughts about work or on my phone and was reacting.

After I realized that pattern and adopted the 3-minute rule, I noticed a marked difference in how I feel and how my kids feel when I enter. The stress of the day changes to joy.
If you also want to adopt that rule, first acknowledge and recognize your pattern.

When you come home, how do you enter? Do you criticize as soon as you enter? How does that make you and your kids feel? Think about the last time you went out of town and came back after some time.

Was your entrance different?

Did you hug and kiss everyone and ask how their day/week went, or did you start critiquing their habits as soon as you entered? You may still be doing that, but usually, a person's typical daily behavior versus behavior after being away is quite different.

From now on, each time you come home, no matter how long you've been away, take a minute before entering. Clear any urgent messages on your phone, then put it away. Clear thoughts about work and coworkers or whatever happened that day.

Take a breath and tell yourself that you are going to meet *the most important people* in your life after a whole day, and make an intention of "no criticism" for 3 minutes.

Then, open the door, call the kids (or family members), hug them, ask them how their day went and listen to them without any criticism. Do you think it would change the way you and your family members feel?

Natasha is a perfectionist, so she was getting trapped in the tendency to focus on other people's weaknesses since they would not do the job as well as she expected.

She intentionally started looking at simple significances in what people do because those things were routine, so they did not typically get noticed.

When she started noticing them, she changed her approach.

She started telling herself that everyone has strengths and weaknesses. She tried to strengthen the strengths and weaken the weaknesses. Her team became a winning team.

She learned the art of constructive criticism from the Toast Master's sandwich technique. In that technique, you bring attention to a strength first, then discuss the weakness with a practical suggestion for improvement, followed by encouraging feedback.

It is called the sandwich technique because the criticism with suggestions for improvement is sandwiched between two genuinely positive pieces of feedback. It becomes much more palatable.

Her gratitude journal practice that had helped her during the initial phase of her journey of stress to joy continued to help her in good times as well.

In times of stress (red light on the road of life), it was allowing her to shift focus from what was missing to what was there. In times of joy, it helped her increase the contentment of heart and peace of mind.

If you would like to use this powerful tool, all you have to do is keep a small diary or notebook by your bed, in your pocket, or in your purse.

Every morning, before you get busy with the daily demands of your life, pick up the journal and write:

IGF (I am Grateful For): Write whatever you feel grateful for that day. It could be as simple as your eyes and hands, or your relations or your achievements.
I usually end my list by saying, "and many uncountable blessings." You already learned this in greater detail in chapter three.

AGF (Advanced Gratitude For): Visualize what you want in life or where you want to be and write it after this prompt. You can say, "I offer advanced gratitude that I am successful, happy, healthy, etc."

Be specific and see in your mind's eye how it would feel when you achieve what you want. You learned this technique in more detail in chapter one.

After doing the gratitude journal for some time, you may use a different version of journaling that focuses on the significance of simple things in life called **3GT/LFT**. Let me share it here.

3GT/LFT: I learned this variation of the gratitude journal from my friend Jean Tracy. For her daily gratitude, she writes **3GT** (Three Good Things) that happened the previous day and **LFT** (Looking Forward To) things she intends for the present day.

When she taught me this method, she said that her 3GT for that day was having a great time with her family, a good night's sleep, and the completion of a project. Her LFT that day was meeting me, feeling good health-wise, and working on her new hobby.

These writing prompt tools will help you to be grateful every day, no matter what the color is on your road of life.

You can access this unique spin on a gratitude journal by downloading the worksheets I've created for you at http://stresstojoy.com/resources

- **IGF**: **I** am **G**rateful **F**or
- **AGF**: (I offer) **A**dvanced **G**ratitude **F**or
- **3GT**: **3 G**ood **T**hings (that happened)
- **LFT**: (I am) **L**ooking **F**orward **T**o

Use one or a combination of these prompts or whatever other prompts you like. The purpose is to bring the focus on what is present in your life and appreciate the significance of simple things that you may be taking for granted. It will help you focus on what is working more than what is not.

You will notice that it will be like changing the color of your lenses. You'll be able to change from dark lenses that put everything in a gloomy tint to bright lenses that allow you to see the brighter side of life.

You will be able to enjoy simple things and increase the level of your joy.

What does S stand for in the happiness acronym of COMPASS?
Significance-focused thinking.

This is when you appreciate and have an attitude of gratitude for simple yet **significant** gifts that you take for granted, both in yourself and others.

If you don't appreciate and express your gratitude, sometimes you realize the importance of things after you lose them. If you don't enjoy small steps along the way, you may reach the top of the mountain but lose the ability to enjoy the passage. If you develop an attitude of gratitude, you will experience joy and peace all the time.

So, if you want to increase the joy in your life, pick up your journal and start your gratitude today. Become generous in expressing your appreciation and gratitude to people around you.

Pause for one minute before entering your home and remind yourself that you are going to meet the most important people in your life.

Pause before entering your work and focus on the significance of your work and coworkers.

COMPASS- Second S

Natasha also realized that there were times that she was getting preoccupied with her problems, her life, and her issues, which was decreasing her joy in life.

As she contemplated, she realized that some of it was caused by the competitiveness of today's meritocratic society.

She valued being the best, and there was nothing wrong about that, but extremes in anything are not good. She tried to look for solutions and found that she felt better when she served others.

Think about a time when someone helped you and made a difference in your life. How did you feel? Did you feel good? Now reverse it. Think about a time when you helped someone and made a difference in her life. How did you feel? Did you feel good?

When you make a difference in someone's life, the smile and gratitude on his face can give you happiness like nothing else.

You feel uplifted. You feel happy from inside.

The more happiness you give, the more you get.

Once, a woman who was searching for happiness went to a Buddhist monk and asked what she could do to fill the emptiness she feels.

He said to bring a smile to others. She was dumbfounded since she was asking for a smile for herself, but the medicine was to bring smiles to others.

I see the benefit when my patients volunteer. It gives them a sense of meaning and engagement. The research on happiness finds that the most long-lasting happiness comes from meaning and engagement.

When human beings express care and love, a neurotransmitter called oxytocin is released into the brain that makes them feel good.

When people serve the community, there are often hurdles. Some people say that they don't get appreciated.

If you focus on the inner feeling you get by helping someone, the satisfaction is the reward in itself.

When I hear people say, "I don't have any major thing to offer," I remember the smile of an old friend's daughter.

She had cerebral palsy.

She could not move, eat, or talk. One day, I went to her room, and she gave me this big smile. Some 20+ years later, I can still see that smile in my mind's eye. She inspired me that day.

If a person who can't take care of herself, who can't even talk, can make this much difference in my life, just imagine what you can do to make a difference in others' lives.

When I start feeling inadequate, I get inspired by the image of a firefly called Jugnu in Urdu. There's a story of Jugnu and a bird from the Urdu poet Allama Iqbal called "Hamdardi." The story is about a bird who finds himself stranded in the dark after searching for food the whole day.

As he is crying, a tiny Jugnu (firefly) shows up. It says, "Don't worry. Although I am small, I have the gift of light. I will light your way home."

I believe that everyone has a light. You have a light. Find that light and light someone's path. You won't have to look for happiness. Joy and peace will find you.

The first habit to happiness in our acronym COMPASS was Compassion for self in addition to others. We discussed that you couldn't fill other peoples' buckets if your bucket is empty. But as your bucket fills, share your blessings, learnings, and happiness with others. Instead of complaining about not getting, start giving and maximize your level of happiness.

So, what does the second **S** stand for in our happiness acronym, COMPASS? **Service**.

You can nurture this habit by identifying your gifts and sharing them for the benefit of others. Being able to serve, itself is your reward. You can serve in the form of giving your smile, your time to listen, or your knowledge.

When you don't give any space for service in your life, you will feel a certain kind of emptiness. If you do, you will feel happiness and peace.

If you are already doing this, continue. If not, commit to doing a good deed every day to make a difference in someone's life.

Similar to the girls' guide/scout motto, "One good deed a day," you may have learned this as a child, but may have a hard time remembering it as an adult.

In summary, if you combine these seven happiness habits, it makes a nice acronym to remember: **COMPASS**.

As a compass faces the right direction, these happiness habits will keep you moving in the right direction.

Conclusion:

*How to bring it together
for your health and happiness.*

Congratulations.

You achieved the goal of reading this book.

You have revisited or learned many tools and techniques as you went through this journey of stress to joy.

The preparation may have taken some time, but the shift in perspective happens in an instant.

You may have already experienced many of these transformational shifts while reading the book.

In addition, you have learned practices that may require a few minutes a day but will have profound long-lasting effects on your health and happiness.

You have added these tools to your toolkit to restore peace of mind. Now, are you going to use them and change your life?

This question reminds me of a common joke about my profession. It goes this way:

"Do you know how many psychiatrists it takes to change a light bulb?

Only one. But it depends if the bulb wants to change."

So, my friend, you can change, but only if you want to. *You* are in control.

When you are learning to drive, the steering wheel is in *your* hands. You have control of the accelerator and the brake.

The instructor is only there to guide you. Similarly, you have to practice what you learn. The guide can show you, but you have to walk the path.

> You are in control of the
> steering wheel of your life.
> Grab it with both hands!

In summary, you have a powerful system that you can apply to any life situation to minimize stress and maximize joy.

Whether it be a stressful situation like surviving a move, a wedding, illness, a natural disaster, a job stress, relationship stress, or just routine life, you now have the tools to tackle them. No matter what color the light is on the road of life, you can transform your feelings from stress to joy by taking the three steps: **ACR**.

First Step—Acknowledge: You acknowledge by becoming aware of how you are feeling, assessing the severity, and acknowledging how you want to feel and why.

Second Step—Calm: You can calm down with mindfulness and meditation. These activities help you relax, increase awareness, and lead to reflective thinking.

Third Step—Reflect: You reflect by writing or expressing in other creative ways.
In your reflection (journaling or talking to a friend, family member, or therapist), you can use the formula: **3R with CPR. Recognize, Realize, and Respond with CPR.**

R1—Recognize: You recognize what is not in your control. Stressors that are coming from outside of you are outside your circle of influence. How you react is in your control, and you can influence what happens next by focusing on aspects that are in your circle of influence.

R2—Realize: You realize the underlying thoughts and beliefs that make you react in a certain manner. When you change those underlying beliefs, your reaction also changes. You realized that beliefs like "you should have control" or that "your life will never be better" are defeating you. You explore the alternative thoughts that make you feel better and replace the thoughts that don't work.

R3—Respond: You respond by facing your situation with intention. You use your wise mind and respond with the most appropriate option. You focus on your priorities and what is inside your circle of influence.

To ensure that your new healthy habits are established, you use the second part of the formula **CPR: Choose, Practice, and Reinforce.**

C—Choose Consciously: You choose to change or continue your response and declare your choice in writing.

P—Practice with persistence: You practice your chosen response enough times to change the programming of your brain's computer and build new pathways. You create an environment conducive to your new practice.

R—Reinforce: You reinforce these patterns with reminders and rewards and increase the chances of a healthy response in the future. As the stress starts to calm, you can practice happiness habits using **COMPASS**:

C—Compassion
O—Open-mindedness
M—Mindfulness
P—Purpose-focused thinking
A—Attitude of acceptance and gratitude
S—Significance focus
S—Service

You will notice that if you don't take steps to manage your stress, it will manage you. Unmanaged stress will cause physical and mental illnesses, add to decreasing your focus and productivity, and steal your joy.

If you manage stress before it manages you, you will feel the freedom from stress. If you develop your happiness habits, you will be able to fully enjoy your life.

As you traverse the journey, watch out for slipping into old habits. Many people start a practice, feel better, and stop practicing.

They slip back into old habits, and their problems recur. Imagine someone who started working out and lost a lot of excess weight, improved her fitness level, and had a lot more energy.

What would happen if she stopped working out? Her hard-earned results would slip away.

The same rule applies to *mental* fitness.

If you apply and continue the practice of exercises that helped you in this program, 75% of your stress issues will resolve. If there are issues that are still lingering, don't hesitate to get external help.

No one is perfect. So, if you are getting small benefits the first time, keep trying. Each time, you will get a further benefit.

If the new habits are working for you, then continue with them. Master them by practicing, writing, and sharing.

Spreading the benefit to others will not only benefit the people you care about but also help you further deepen the skill. If not, you need to seek additional help from someone who can customize the process for you.

Whether by yourself or with additional help, try, try, and try again until you succeed.

One of my patients commits to making one change and then practicing it for a month, then adds another change the following month, so he keeps improving without overwhelming himself with too many changes.

So, make your plan of action today because, as Aldous Huxley said, "There's only one corner of the universe you can be certain of improving, and that is you. You have to begin there, not outside, and not on other people."

Write down one change you plan to make in your life today, and write this prompt in your journal: "I commit myself to…"

Today is the first day of the rest of your life.
How the rest of your life goes will be
determined by the decisions you make today.

Make the best decisions.

If you don't, the stressors of life will cause
stress and suffering. If you practice the skills of
reducing stress and nurturing happiness that
you have learned here, you will continue your
transformation from stress to joy.

Thank you for investing the time in your
personal development and choosing me to be
your guide. I am grateful for the privilege.

To your happy, healthy, and harmonious life!

Until next time,

Dr. Rozina

Appendix

Stress to Joy (STJ)
Condensed
Reminder card

ACR- Basic Steps
A: Acknowledge your feelings
C: Calm down with mindfulness and meditation
R: Reflect with effective tools (writing, talking or thinking through)

3 R- Formula for Reflection
R1: Recognize (your role)
R2: Realize: underlying Thoughts, Attitudes and Beliefs
R3: Respond: with your wise mind

CPR- Make Healthy Habits.
C: Choose your focus and declare
P: Practice with reminders
R: Reinforce with rewards

Exercises by chapter:

Chapter 1:

1. Emotional Coping Account (ECA) balance sheet and deposit list to rapidly assess and improve emotional balance and resilience..
2. AGF: Advanced Gratitude to harness power of visualization without logical mind questioning

Chapter 2:

3. Mindfulness to improve calm and focus
4. Mindful Driving to calm and decrease driving stress.
5. Meditation different types to calm busy mind
6. Feet to Floor – 1-minute relaxation exercise for busy people
7. Active Meditation to calm active minds
8. Art Meditation to calm creative minds

Chapter 3:

9. Self-Dialogue Journal-a technique to get out of your own way and connect with inner wisdom
10. Gratitude Journal-a technique to shift focus and feel the joy no matter what.

11. Therapeutic Writing- a technique to empty the mental garbage bin.

Chapter 4:
12. Formula: 3R with CPR to reflect in most effective manner and establish healthy habits.
13. Circle of Influence to stop wasting energy on matters outside your influence.
14. 90/10 Principle to focus on the matters that matter.

Chapter 5:
15. Crossroad Technique to overcome worrying
16. CBT: 3-Column Technique to Identify and modify underlying thoughts and beliefs

Chapter 6:
17. Using Wise Mind to tap the inner wisdom despite the pull of rational and emotional mind in different directions.
18. Brain Dump Bubbles to find sanity in unending todo lists
19. 5 Ds for Prioritizing
20. Quadrant Thinking to sort through multiple demands

Further Resource
Stress to Joy Online Course

Now that you have read the book or listened to the audiobook, you may wish to download several free resources at http://stresstojoy.com/resources.

Do you want to master stress to joy skills even further? Keep reading to hear what people requested along with my responses.

Sam said;
"I am an audio/visual learner. I learn better when I see and hear things"
The video course may help you that you can listen or watch anywhere, anytime.
http://stresstojoy.com/online-course

"I learn better in small increments because I don't have too much time."
You'll see that each of my videos are limited to bite size sessions of 5-15 min each.

"It takes me time to change my habits."
This video course is for 21 days, the usual time for someone to establish new habits.

263

"I learn better when I see examples of how to apply certain techniques in various situations" You'll find many stories from practical life to help you apply the tools.

The second week is dedicated to applying the Stress to Joy techniques when you are having specific stress reactions.

These could be feeling tense and overwhelmed, difficulties sleeping due to a racing mind, emotional problems like increased irritability and worrying, or self-sabotaging behaviors like emotional eating.

"Sometimes my stress level is low, how do I continue to improve my resilience and happiness?"

You will find more detail in each of the seven happiness habits with many practical examples in week three. They will prepare you for any situation life presents to you. You will enjoy life more fully too.

Rene stated;
"I learn better and faster when I write and do things."

You will find worksheets with prompts to
stimulate your thinking.
Write down your ideas.
Practice them.

This will help you integrate the techniques.
*"I want something tangible that I can refer back
to in future."*

With the worksheets at the end of each video,
you will be creating your own 100-page
activity guide.

It will be your personal reference for
maintaining the stress-free skills whenever
you need them.

Natasha said, *"I like to listen to the audios while I
drive."*
The video is also in an audio format to listen to
while you commute.

*"I know intellectually what mindfulness means
but I'd like someone to walk me through steps on
how to practice being mindful in my daily life."*

You may use the 21 bonus audios to guide you
through practicing mindfulness during simple
daily activities like chores, shower, walking,
driving etc.

Each guide is only 1-3 minutes, so you could easily listen to it in the morning and then practice mindfulness while you do that activity during the day. After 21 days of practice, you'll find mindfulness easier and more automatic. Make it your intention.

All these solutions have morphed into the Online Video Course: "Stress to Joy in 21 days." And you can benefit from it by downloading it now at: http://stresstojoy.com/online-course

Some of the early participants of this course gave the following feedback:

"The 21 Day Stress to Joy course is a game changer. I learned so much about how I think and the changes I can make in my own attitude that will help me be a happier person, a better influence on my children, and an overall positive member of society. The guided journaling is a great way to remember all of the

positive things in my life, instead of just 'getting out' the negative things that happened that day." **Kaja Knight.**

"The course is amazing. The way you present feels so natural with the smile in your voice, like you are sitting across from me and talking to me. The way you convey your messages in an easy to understand manner shows the countless other patients that have been through variations of the program and the number of iterations it has gone through." **Shana**

"Thank you, Dr. Rozina, for helping me balance my emotional bank account! As a registered nurse and student, I'm no stranger to stress. Your online course has made me rethink about how I react to stressful situations. With heart and humor, you've shown me how to relax, sleep better, prioritize amid seemingly overwhelming choices, and let go of what I can't control.

Little by little I'm developing a 'wise mind' to act more in line with my life's purpose. These teachings require practice, but already I'm living more mindfully, self-aware, and reflecting love in my relationships. May you always be happy and grateful." **Ken Dyer RN**

"You can move from Stress to Joy even if you're stressed, worried or worn out. Take Dr. Rozina's 21-Day video course, she'll teach you how to move from stress to joy with easy step-by-step solutions. I find that starting each morning with one of her brief videos, I'm relaxed and ready to face the day.

The worksheets help me practice the changes I need. If you're like me, you'll love her clear approach to becoming a more relaxed and happier person. Thank you, Dr. Rozina!"
Jean Tracy MSS

"Dr. Rozina's Stress to Joy course is an awesome starting point for systematically eliminating overwhelm in your life! She shares some great fundamental ideas, models and concepts to help you to rewire your brain for happiness first.

The toolbox presented in this course is practical and you can begin implementing it into your daily life immediately. Her positive energy came though the video modules as a pleasant surprise every day throughout the course.

I'm looking forward to the next one!" **Shakeel Mohammad.**

"Thank you for sharing such great and wonderful videos. Awesomeness!!! The videos covered a lot of information, delivered in concise chunks that were easy to absorb.

The structure is clear, logical, and effective; Dr. Lakhani's voice is sweet and very easy to understand. Her techniques have provided me positive upliftment, compassion, and a tremendous amount of energy.

I work as an ER physician, and through these lessons, I have improved my focusing in high-pressure situations. I particularly love how Dr. Lakhani explains the formula for Reflection-3R, tips on how to let go of worrying and prevent suffering twice, and 5D techniques to overcome overwhelming situation.

Dr. Lakhani put a lot of thought and expertise into designing these techniques." **Dr. Khairunn Rajwani.**

"Your 21-day course helped me finally understand the joy of life. You made this course so clear and easy to understand.

You have no idea how much you have helped me to cope up with my stress and enjoy mindfulness.

It has helped change my life at a point when I needed it the most.

I would recommend it to anyone. It is one of those things that you highlight and go back to review parts of it again. I love positive energy on your face on each and every video of your course.

Your book and online course is truly out there for a great cause." **Salima Hasnani**

If you would like to find similar benefits, decrease your stress and enjoy your life more, you can start this 21-day program today by getting our instant download at: http://stresstojoy.com/online-course

If it helps decrease your pain and suffering and increase your happiness, I will be pleased, and my mission will be accomplished.

~ Dr. Rozina Lakhani

Love this book?

Please tell me how this book helped you by leaving a review. Share it with your family, friends and colleagues too. Together let's decrease stress, increase happiness, and promote love in the world.

If you would like further information about online consultation, live events or speaking engagements, please contact support@drrozina.com or visit https://DrRozina.com.